THE WEALTH LADDER

THE
WEALTH
LADDER

PROVEN STRATEGIES FOR EVERY STEP
OF YOUR FINANCIAL LIFE

NICK MAGGIULLI

PORTFOLIO | PENGUIN

Portfolio / Penguin
An imprint of Penguin Random House LLC
1745 Broadway, New York, NY 10019
penguinrandomhouse.com

Most Portfolio books are available at a discount when purchased in quantity
for sales promotions or corporate use. Special editions, which include
personalized covers, excerpts, and corporate imprints, can be created when
purchased in large quantities. For more information, please call (212) 572-2232
or e-mail specialmarkets@penguinrandomhouse.com. Your local bookstore
can also assist with discounted bulk purchases using the Penguin Random House
corporate Business-to-Business program. For assistance in locating a
participating retailer, e-mail B2B@penguinrandomhouse.com.

BOOK DESIGN BY TANYA MAIBORODA

ISBN 9780593854037 (hardcover)
ISBN 9780593854044 (ebook)
ISBN 9798217048595 (international edition)

Printed in the United States of America

1st Printing

The authorized representative in the EU for product safety and compliance is
Penguin Random House Ireland, Morrison Chambers, 32 Nassau Street,
Dublin D02 YH68, Ireland, https://eu-contact.penguin.ie.

To my father,
For teaching me the game.
Don't move until you see it.

CONTENTS

INTRODUCTION

When I was five years old my father taught me how to play chess. For fun, he'd invite his friends over and have them challenge me to a game. They were always shocked when I won. Picture it. You're twenty-seven years old and a kindergartner just crushed your self-esteem with a single word—checkmate. Jokes aside, I wasn't a future chess prodigy. My father's friends were simply terrible at the game.

I stopped playing chess a few years later when my parents split up and didn't pick it up again until my junior year of high school. I found a renewed interest in the game after playing against a friend, and we decided to start a chess club. To improve my skills, I spent hours studying openings and the best ways to respond to them. My first five to ten moves in a game were often automatic, pulled from memory. My strategy worked and I got better. But it wasn't until I entered my first real chess competition that I learned an unforgettable lesson.

When amateurs learn chess, many of them do the same

things I did. They memorize openings and hope that their opponent makes a mistake along the way. They win based on good initial positioning and by avoiding simple blunders.

But Victor, one of the star players at my first chess competition, was different. He didn't play chess like an amateur. Sometimes Victor would start a game with a traditional opening and sometimes he wouldn't. He'd accept a gambit (the sacrifice of a piece) with one opponent, but completely ignore it with another. It was like he wasn't playing the same game as the rest of us.

Here's the puzzling part though—no matter how much I watched him play, I couldn't figure out how he did it. I had no frame of reference for his decision making. You'd think that if I kept practicing, I'd eventually be able to compete with Victor, but you'd be wrong. I could not simply take my approach of going through chess openings, do it for hundreds of additional hours, and get to his skill level. My strategy plus time did not equal Victor.

No, what I really needed was to find a different way to play chess altogether. This is the lesson Victor taught me: Sometimes effort alone doesn't determine your results. How and where you apply that effort does.

Years later, I realized that the same thing is true when it comes to building wealth. Having the wrong framework when trying to get ahead financially can leave you spinning your wheels with little to show for it. Many people try to fix this by working more hours or following the latest financial advice, but they still don't see a big change. Then they attribute their lack of success to their work ethic, their boss, or bad luck, when their problem has been their approach all along. They're trying to memorize openings while the Victors of the world pass them by. As Andy Grove, the former CEO of Intel, once said, "There are so many people working so hard and achieving so little."[1] Their problem isn't effort—it's strategy.

But what if there was a better way? What if there was a new framework for understanding how to build wealth, one that actually worked? Not a get-rich-quick scheme or a one-size-fits-all solution to your money problems, but a new philosophy for thinking about money altogether. What if this system didn't tell you *what to do*, but taught you *how to think* about your finances? Telling people what to do works fine when they face the same problem again and again. But, this approach doesn't work with money and wealth, where things are constantly in flux. Interest rates change, our careers change, and our desires change, so why should our strategy for building wealth stay the same? It shouldn't. Instead, a better approach would be to have a solid framework to rely upon throughout our long and varied lives.

That framework is what I call the Wealth Ladder.

If I gave you $100, would that change your life? How about $100,000? What about $100 million? Your answer will depend upon a variety of factors, but most importantly, how much money you have *today*. For most people, $100 million would fundamentally transform their lifestyle. But for someone like Jeff Bezos, $100 million wouldn't even register. This simple observation has profound implications for understanding wealth, and how our view of it can change as we acquire more of it.

For the record, when I say "wealth" I am referring to your net worth, or your assets minus your liabilities. That is everything you own (i.e., property, financial assets, cash, etc.) minus everything that you owe to others (i.e., mortgage, student loans, credit card debt, etc.). The problem is, we've been looking at wealth in the wrong way. We've assumed that more wealth is better and that it can solve all our problems. We've also assumed that more wealth means more personal consumption. Unfortunately, this is only true in the extremes.

The person with $100,000 can afford a lifestyle that is quite different from the person with only $1,000. However, the person with $500,000 lives nearly identically to the person with $400,000. Though these two people are separated by $100,000, they likely shop at similar stores, drive similar cars, and live in similar homes. In this sense, our enjoyment of wealth isn't something that goes up with every additional dollar (or $1,000) we get, but something that increases in steps.

In this sense, wealth isn't a straight line, it's a ladder. And each rung of this ladder corresponds with a wealth level that will impact nearly every facet of your financial life. From how you spend money, to how you earn it and how you invest it, each level of the Wealth Ladder is unique. What are these wealth levels?

- **LEVEL 1** (<$10,000)
- **LEVEL 2** ($10,000–$100,000)
- **LEVEL 3** ($100,000–$1 million)
- **LEVEL 4** ($1 million–$10 million)
- **LEVEL 5** ($10 million–$100 million)
- **LEVEL 6** ($100 million+)

The levels are separated by a factor of 10, because this corresponds with the increase in wealth needed to create a large lifestyle change. You can see these wealth levels with their respective net worth ranges in the chart below.

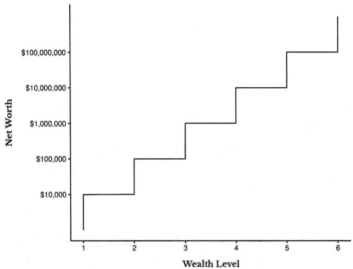

Wealth Level Based on Net Worth

For example, Level 1 is for those with a net worth less than $10,000, Level 2 is for those with a net worth of $10,000 to $100,000, and so on.

From this we can infer that each level up the Wealth Ladder is exponentially more difficult to reach than the one before it. This explains why the number of people around the world in each level tends to get smaller as we go further up the ladder. For example, the following chart is a breakdown of the percentage of people in each wealth level around the world[2] and in the United States[3] as of 2023:

Wealth Level	Share of Adults (World)	Number of Adults (World)	Share of Households (US)	Number of Households (US)
Level 1 (<$10k)	39.5%	1.49B	18%	24M
Level 2 ($10k–$100k)	43%	1.61B	21%	28M
Level 3 ($100k–$1M)	16%	613M	43%	56M
Level 4 ($1M–$10M)	1.4%*	54M*	16.3%	21M
Level 5 ($10M–$100M)	0.099625%*	4M*	1.6925%	2M
Level 6 ($100M+)	0.000375%	30,000	0.0075%	10,000

*Extrapolated from U.S. data

As you can see, the majority of people around the world fall in Levels 1–2, with increasingly smaller groups of people in each level above that. There are roughly 1.5 billion adults in Level 1 (<$10k), but there are only about thirty thousand adults in Level 6 ($100M+). Given the amount of wealth concentrated in the United States, the distribution of people across the Wealth Ladder is shifted upward here. As a result, most households in the U.S. are in Level 3 ($100k–$1M), not Levels 1–2. Despite this upward shift, there are still far more households lower on the Wealth Ladder than higher. For example, there are 56 million U.S. households in Level 3, but only about 10,000 U.S. households in Level 6.

Since such immense fortunes are rare, some people have

warped perceptions of wealth and what it means to do well financially. If we map the different economic classes in the U.S. onto the Wealth Ladder, we can see this more clearly:

- **LEVEL 1**. Lower class (<$10k)
- **LEVEL 2**. Working class ($10k–$100k)
- **LEVEL 3**. Middle class ($100k–$1M)
- **LEVEL 4**. Upper middle class ($1M–$10M)
- **LEVEL 5**. Upper class ($10M–$100M)
- **LEVEL 6**. The superrich ($100M+)

From this perspective, you can begin to understand why some people with lots of money don't feel rich—it's because they're looking at higher economic classes or Wealth Levels. People in Level 4 look at people in Levels 5–6 and say, "I'm not rich, *they* are rich." Though people in Level 4 are millionaires, they can't afford to live like the stereotypical rich person depicted in the media and popular culture. Those people, who are in Levels 5–6, can actually afford to fly in private jets and own supercars.

From this simple categorization of wealth into levels, we can also imagine how your financial strategy might change as you move up the Wealth Ladder. For example, the strategy to get you from Level 1 to Level 2 will be fundamentally different from the strategy to get you from Level 5 to Level 6. Throughout this book I will refer to these strategies based on the level they will help you in (e.g., this is a Level 2 strategy).

This categorization of wealth into levels also explains why different financial experts give seemingly contradictory advice.

One may argue that budgeting is the key to financial success, while another claims that starting a business is more important. Who is right? The Wealth Ladder teaches us that both of them are, *they are just talking to people at different levels on the Wealth Ladder.*

While budgeting can be useful for someone in Level 1 of the Wealth Ladder, it likely won't make a difference for someone in Level 6. This would classify budgeting as Level 1 strategy. Similarly, starting and scaling a business could help someone in Level 6 build more wealth, but probably isn't the right strategy for someone in Level 1. This would classify running a business as a higher-level strategy. Just like a fitness coach would provide different diet and exercise advice to an obese person than to a well-trained athlete, the Wealth Ladder will provide different financial advice based on where you are on your financial journey.

In this way, the Wealth Ladder is a grand unifying framework that will fundamentally change how you think about wealth and how to build it. Once you've grasped the concept of the Wealth Ladder, it will be difficult to look at your finances the same way again. As the saying goes, "Once you see it, you can't unsee it." Your shift in thinking will influence how you choose a career, how you take risks, and, ultimately, how you live your life. You'll see that the difference between those who build wealth and those who don't isn't necessarily how hard they work. Rather, it's what strategies they follow and where they focus their time and energy. Thankfully, you won't need to guess about where to focus yours. The Wealth Ladder already has the answer.

Before we start climbing *The Wealth Ladder*, let me tell you a little bit about my story. We'll go deeper later, but here's the highlight reel.

I grew up in a working-class family in Southern California. My mom was a loan processor. My dad bounced between jobs—limo driver, insurance agent, and more. They divorced when I was young and declared bankruptcy multiple times before I turned eighteen.

This unfortunate set of circumstances meant I had no financial role models. No road map. I had to figure out money on my own. I became the first in my family to graduate from college—and not just any college. I went to Stanford, an elite private school where I met people from different walks of life, many wildly different from my own.

From there, I started my career in litigation consulting, working alongside high-powered professionals across the business world. For a few years, I even played in a band with a handful of lawyers. Now, I work at Ritholtz Wealth Management, a firm that manages more than $5 billion in assets for thousands of clients. I'm also a financial writer and author of the bestselling book *Just Keep Buying*.

Because of these experiences, I've seen wealth from every angle. I've met people at every level of *The Wealth Ladder*. I've also analyzed an enormous amount of financial data—everything from the Survey of Consumer Finances (run by the Federal Reserve) to the University of Michigan's Panel Study of Income Dynamics, and more. These datasets contain financial information on tens of thousands of US households over the span of five decades. *The Wealth Ladder* distills what I've learned from this research along with my own journey with money.

Most importantly, I've built life-changing wealth—for myself, my family, and for thousands of people around the world—because of it. *The Wealth Ladder* is the framework I've developed to help you do the same. And while I'm not at the highest wealth level, I know many who are. Some are my mentors. Some were colleagues. Some I've met online. I've seen the benefits of great wealth—but also its pitfalls.

This book is both a guide and a warning. It's about how to build wealth—and knowing when enough is enough. My goal? To help you climb *The Wealth Ladder* in a way that actually improves your life. The only question left is: Are you ready to climb it?

THE WEALTH LADDER

PART I

UNDERSTANDING

THE

WEALTH

LADDER

CHAPTER 1

Spending up
the Wealth Ladder

When Cleopatra was the queen of Egypt, she was the richest woman in the world. To entertain her guests, she often threw lavish parties. Following a series of such feasts, Mark Antony, the Roman general, remarked that she hosted the most extravagant banquets in the world. Wanting to impress Antony even further, Cleopatra claimed that she could spend 10 million sesterces (about $20 million today) on a single meal. Thinking that such a feat was impossible, Antony made a bet with the boastful Cleopatra. The Egyptian queen accepted and claimed that she would prove him wrong the next day.

To keep her promise, the following day Cleopatra had her servants set up a banquet similar to the ones she and Antony had enjoyed in the previous days. But this time Cleopatra wore one of her most prized possessions—a pair of pearl earrings. These weren't just any pearl earrings though. They were considered the largest pearls the ancient world had ever seen.

When Antony arrived at the banquet, he joked that there was no way that it had cost 10 million sesterces. Cleopatra replied that he was correct, and that she would consume the 10 million sesterces herself. To fulfill her promise, Cleopatra had her servants bring out a glass of vinegar strong enough to dissolve pearls. With Antony watching, she removed one of the prized pearls from her earrings, dropped it in the glass, and watched it dissolve before drinking it.[1] As Cleopatra began to remove the pearl from her other earring, Antony conceded that he had lost the bet.

The story of Cleopatra and her pearl earrings highlights the lengths people will go to to flaunt their wealth. But it also illustrates how spending money is relative. There are people like Cleopatra, who can consume vast resources without impacting their wealth. Then there are others who must track every dollar they spend in order to stay afloat. It reminds me of the time Jay-Z said, "What's fifty grand to a mother****er like me? Can you please remind me?" When Jay wrote those lyrics in 2011, he had an estimated net worth of $450 million. This means that, at the time, "fifty grand" represented about 0.01 percent (or 1/10,000th) of Jay-Z's fortune.

This data point might seem random, but 0.01 percent of your net worth is actually a great proxy for what constitutes a trivial amount of money for you. For example, if you have a net worth of $10,000, paying $1 more (or 0.01 percent more) for something shouldn't have any long-term impact on your finances. Similarly, if you have a net worth of $100,000, you should be able to pay $10 more for an item without skipping a beat. I call this the 0.01% Rule ("the Point Zero One Percent Rule").

Using the 0.01% Rule as a guide, we can demonstrate how

the Wealth Ladder relates to spending money. To do this, I've listed the six levels of the Wealth Ladder below and how they relate to different spending categories:

- **LEVEL 1.** Paycheck-to-paycheck (<$10k): You are conscious of every dollar you spend. This includes people with crippling debt.
- **LEVEL 2.** Grocery freedom ($10k–$100k): You can buy what you want at the grocery store without worrying about your finances.
- **LEVEL 3.** Restaurant freedom ($100k–$1M): You can eat what you want at restaurants.
- **LEVEL 4.** Travel freedom ($1M–$10M): You travel when and where you want.
- **LEVEL 5.** House freedom ($10M–$100M): You can afford your dream home with little impact on your overall finances.
- **LEVEL 6.** Impact freedom ($100M+): You can use money to have a profound impact on the lives of others (e.g., buy businesses, engage in large-scale philanthropy, etc.).

What's interesting about the intersection of the Wealth Ladder with spending is that you quickly realize that certain sums of money won't improve your life in any noticeable way. For example, for the typical person in Level 3 ($100k–$1M), an extra $10,000 won't move them to Level 4. This isn't enough to free someone from considering the cost of lodging and transportation (i.e., travel freedom) for the rest of their life. However, that same $10,000 given to someone in Level 1 will likely get them to Level 2, unless they are deeply in debt. The same amount of money given to people on different levels of the Wealth Ladder will have a drastically different impact on their lives.

The reason why the Wealth Ladder integrates so well with each spending category listed above is because of the 0.01% Rule. In each level, a single spending decision represents about 0.01 percent of the net worth level shown. For example, let's say you are at the grocery store deciding whether to purchase a dozen eggs for $3.99 or a dozen cage-free eggs for $4.99. If your net worth is $100, this single choice (paying $1 extra for cage-free eggs) would have a large impact on your finances, as it represents 1 percent of your total wealth. However, if you were worth over $10,000, the decision to spend $1 more on cage-free eggs would be relatively unimportant to your finances. In other words, if you're worth $10,000, an extra dollar on eggs won't change your life, but if you're worth $100, it might.

In this case, by having more than $10,000 you would have reached the initial stages of Level 2 ("Grocery freedom"). You can start to buy whatever you want at the grocery store. As you gain more wealth, you gain more grocery freedom. By the time you have $100,000 in wealth (the beginning of Level 3), you should have complete freedom to buy what you want at the grocery store.

We can continue extending this idea up the Wealth Ladder to ever more expensive spending categories. For example, imagine you are in a restaurant, where you are deciding between a burger for $20 and salmon for $30. If your net worth exceeds $100,000, then that $10 difference in price is trivial (i.e., it's less than 0.01 percent of your net worth). This means you have reached Level 3 ("Restaurant freedom"). If you continue to scale the logic of the 0.01% Rule upward, you will see that the impact of a single spending decision within each Wealth Level is as follows:

THE 0.01% RULE

- **LEVEL 1** (<$10k). Paycheck-to-paycheck: $0.01–$0.99 per decision
- **LEVEL 2** ($10k–$100k). Grocery freedom: $1–$9 per decision
- **LEVEL 3** ($100k–$1M). Restaurant freedom: $10–$99 per decision
- **LEVEL 4** ($1M–$10M). Travel freedom: $100–$999 per decision
- **LEVEL 5** ($10M–$100M). House freedom: $1,000–$9,999 per decision
- **LEVEL 6** ($100M+). Impact freedom: $10,000+ per decision

You can see this in the chart on the following page, which illustrates by wealth level how much additional spending someone could have without impacting their finances.

From this perspective, you realize that many people in the same wealth level have similar consumption patterns. Even people in adjacent wealth levels consume in roughly similar ways. For example, people in Level 4 have a lifestyle very much like those in Level 3. Yes, those in Level 4 may have a nicer car or a bigger house, but they don't have a chauffeur. They may buy slightly fancier food or upgrade to business class more often, but they don't fly private. Despite their 10x difference in wealth, people in Level 4 live in a way that is familiar to people in Level 3. This is why Level 4 is considered upper middle class and Level 3 is considered middle class. Both have similar lifestyles, but one is just slightly fancier.

Of course, exceptions to this general pattern exist. Not

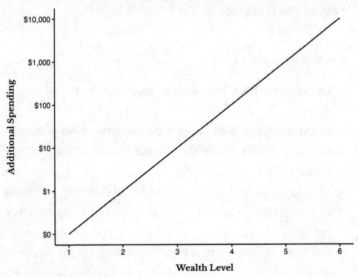

everyone consumes based on their wealth level. You will find those in Level 6 who still fly economy class and hunt for bargains. And you will find those in Level 1 who regularly splurge on dining and travel even when they probably shouldn't.

The primary reason is that many people spend based on their income, not their wealth. This can make sense at first glance. After all, if you have more money coming in, you can have more money going out. But spending based on your income won't necessarily help you climb the Wealth Ladder. For example, if you earn $1 million a year, you can afford to buy cage-free eggs, order fine bottles of wine, and travel first class quite often. However, if you have zero dollars to your name (Level 1), then you shouldn't be doing any of those things. Until you have demonstrated that you can save money, you shouldn't be living such an extravagant lifestyle. On the other hand, if you made $1 million in a year and were able to save $200,000 of it, you've shown some financial responsibility. As a result, that $200,000 would get you to Level 3 of the Wealth Ladder ("Restaurant freedom"), which would let you splurge a little while dining out.

This is why you should spend based on your wealth, not your income. Excluding inheritances, trust funds, and lottery winnings, having wealth demonstrates financial discipline. It illustrates that you have control over your spending and that you know how to save money. Without such control, you could end up in a bad place financially. For example, if you consume based solely on your income, any disruption to that income could send your finances into a tailspin.

Unfortunately, most people don't realize this until it's too late. The truth is that income can be fickle. One day you're making good money and the next you're looking for a new job. This can happen to anyone, but it's even more common among those with higher incomes. As researchers at the National Bureau of Economic Research (NBER) discovered, "Positive shocks to high-income individuals are quite transitory, whereas negative shocks are very persistent."[2] In other words, sharp drops in income are more likely to be permanent among higher earners. Unfortunately, these large declines are becoming more common over time as well. As one study found:

> The share of households experiencing a 50 percent plunge in income over a two-year period climbed from about 7 percent in the early 1970s to more than 12 percent in the early 2000s before retreating to 10 percent in the run-up to the Great Recession.[3]

If your lifestyle is fully financed by your income, experiencing such a steep decline in earnings can be jarring. This explains why some professional athletes end up broke even after making millions of dollars a year while playing. Their problem is that they spent money according to their income, not their wealth. Once that income dries up, their financial problems begin. Though the average annual salary across the four major U.S. sports leagues exceeded $4.5 million in 2020, some of these players will still get into financial trouble because of how they spend money.[4]

This is why the Wealth Ladder suggests that you spend money according to your wealth level. If someone is in Level 2 ("Grocery freedom"), they shouldn't be splurging at fancy restaurants, which is reserved for Level 3. If they are in Level 3 ("Restaurant freedom"), they shouldn't be upgrading to business or first class, and so forth. Of course, they may disagree with me and insist that they *need* the finer things in life. But this is just an excuse. In truth, the most expensive thing some people own is their ego.

Believe me, I don't like telling people to cut their spending. The data suggests that this isn't the best way to build wealth in the long run anyway. Raising your income is far more important. We will elaborate on this in future chapters.

On the other hand, people shouldn't overdo their spending either. Spending according to your level won't guarantee that you climb the Wealth Ladder, but you are less likely to fall down it. In this way, the Wealth Ladder provides the perfect balance between allowing you to splurge and limiting excess.

The key here is to think about your spending *above your necessities*. Of course you will need to spend money on food, housing, and a host of other basics. You can't avoid that. But how much more can you spend beyond your needs? That's where the Wealth Ladder comes in. There's a difference between eating for sustenance and buying whatever food you want. There's a difference between flying coach and traveling in style. If we assume that your income pays for your necessities, then your wealth pays for your upgrades.

This works because of the 0.01% Rule. If we assume that your wealth is invested and growing by 0.01 percent *per day* above inflation, this translates into a growth rate of roughly 3.7 percent per year. This is a relatively conservative annual return, even after adjusting for inflation. Assuming that your wealth will grow by 3.7 percent annually, you could spend about 0.01 percent of your wealth each day and maintain the same net worth. For example, if you had $100,000 invested and it grew by 0.01 percent daily, that would give you ten dollars that you could spend *in excess of* your income each day. You could spend this money *without* reducing your long-term wealth. Unfortunately, if you don't have any other income, this won't be much to live on.

This is why spending according to your wealth level generally requires that you have income to live on. For example, if you saved up $20,000 and then suddenly lost your job, you would technically be in Level 2 ("Grocery freedom"). Unfortunately, you won't have all that much freedom when you go to buy groceries. If you can't find another job or income source, that $20,000 would only allow you to spend about $2 per day (or $14 per week) while staying in the same level of wealth. This is the most the 0.01% Rule can offer in this case. Unfortunately, that's nowhere near enough to live on in most developed countries like the United States. As a result, you'd have to either find another income source or spend down your wealth.

This demonstrates that while the Wealth Ladder can act as a guide to how we spend money, we must consider our income as well. Someone with $30,000 in the bank and no job needs to be more cautious about how they spend their money than someone with $10,000 in the bank earning $200,000 a year. The same thing is true for retirees who aren't working anymore. A sixty-five-year-old retiree with a $1 million nest egg can't spend money like an employed thirty-five-year-old with a $1 million investment portfolio. Though they are both at the lower end of Level 4 ("Travel freedom"), the sixty-five-year-old doesn't have that much travel freedom.

But there is an additional layer to this problem that can impact how you spend your money, and it has everything to do with what your wealth is comprised of.

So far, when we've discussed spending up the Wealth Ladder we've used your overall net worth to determine your wealth level. This is what we will do throughout this book. But there is a special consideration we need to make when it comes to spending money. Because, unfortunately, not all wealth is equal when you go to spend it. For example, imagine someone with a net worth of $1.1 million broken down like this:

- $250,000 in a brokerage account
- $250,000 in retirement accounts
- $600,000 in home equity

Based on the Wealth Ladder, this person would be in Level 4 ($1M–$10M), since they have $1.1 million in net worth. However, only a small portion of their net worth is liquid (i.e., can be accessed immediately). How much exactly? Just the $250,000 in their brokerage account. Their $600,000 in home equity and their $250,000 in retirement accounts cannot be easily accessed, so it doesn't count toward their *liquid* net worth. Based on their $250,000 brokerage account, we would classify them as Level 3 ($100k–$1M).

So which is it? Are they Level 3 based on their *liquid* net worth or Level 4 based on their overall net worth? While technically they are in Level 4, given the breakdown of their assets, I would suggest that they spend *as if* they were in Level 3. Why? Because unless they plan on selling their home to get access to their home equity, they should act like it doesn't exist for spending purposes. And even if they do sell their home, it's not like they could spend all that money; after selling their home, they would still need to pay for a place to live. The wealth they gained by selling their home would be partially offset by a new ongoing rental expense. We can make the same argument about their retirement accounts as well. These accounts are technically set aside for *future* spending. By withdrawing from them (and paying the fees to do so), they can spend more now but will spend less later. Therefore, if they want to continue moving up the Wealth Ladder, they should spend based on their liquid net worth ($250,000), not their net worth ($1.1 million). The chart on the following page shows how your spending can vary based on your liquid net worth across the Wealth Ladder.

This illustrates how the composition of your wealth can

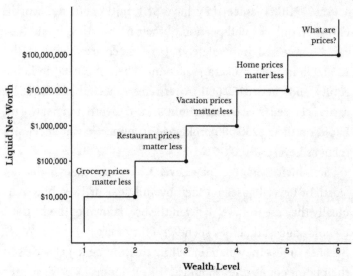

Spending by Wealth Level

Liquid Net Worth (y-axis)

What are prices?

$100,000,000

Home prices matter less

$10,000,000

Vacation prices matter less

$1,000,000

Restaurant prices matter less

$100,000

Grocery prices matter less

$10,000

Wealth Level (x-axis: 1 2 3 4 5 6)

impact your spending. For example, being "house rich, but cash poor" is one scenario where what you have on paper won't help with your day-to-day living expenses. This is because some assets generate income while others reduce expenses. For example, stocks will typically generate income, but a car will reduce your need to pay future transportation expenses. With a car you don't have to call a cab or a ridesharing service (like Uber) every time you want to go somewhere. The same is true of your home. While your primary residence won't generate income, it does allow you to avoid paying the market rate for rent.

Ultimately, the Wealth Ladder can and should be adapted to your financial situation. It's more of an approximate art than an exact science. I say this because the specific amounts I've listed for each level of the Wealth Ladder are not set in stone. Prices will vary over time, across currencies, and in different countries. The specific numbers are not what's important. It's the underlying framework that matters.

For example, imagine what would happen to the Wealth Ladder if, overnight, the price of everything in the economy doubled. What if milk went from $5 to $10 a gallon? What if a car that once cost $20,000 now costs $40,000? In this scenario, Level 1 of the Wealth Ladder would be <$20,000, Level 2 would be $20,000–$200,000, and so forth. While the absolute values of the Wealth Ladder have doubled, on a relative basis, nothing has changed.

The same thing will be true if the prices in one spending category shift dramatically. For example, if a new technology gets invented that significantly reduces the cost of traveling around the world, then Level 4 would probably no longer correspond with "Travel freedom." It would correspond with something else entirely. Instead of getting bogged down with the specifics, focus on the big picture. What's important is *the idea of the Wealth Ladder* and how your spending can increase slowly as you move up it.

Though you may never have the same spending power as Cleopatra, by using the Wealth Ladder you can ensure that your wealth doesn't dissolve before your eyes.

Chapter 1 Summary

- Income is fickle, wealth is less so. Spend based on your wealth, not your income.

- The 0.01% Rule ("the Point Zero One Percent Rule"): The amount you can spend above your income each day while maintaining your wealth is 0.01% (or 1/10,000th) of your net worth.

- You don't need to be frugal to build wealth, but don't overspend either.

- If you have difficulty spending according to your Wealth Level, then the most expensive thing that you own is your ego.

- To be conservative, spend based on your *liquid* net worth rather than your net worth.

- The Wealth Ladder isn't a rigid set of rules, but a loose framework for your spending.

―

Optimizing your spending is just one way you can use the Wealth Ladder to improve your financial decisions. But this framework can also be applied to how you navigate your career as well. For this, we turn to our next chapter on earning up the Wealth Ladder.

CHAPTER 2

Earning up
the Wealth Ladder

You may have not heard of Kōnosuke Matsushita, but he is one of the greatest businessmen in history. Matsushita was born in 1894, the youngest of eight children, and grew up in a farm community south of Osaka, Japan. He got his first job at age fifteen in the electrical industry and was promoted multiple times within a few years. By age twenty-two, he was an inspector, the highest paid position available to him.

Though Matsushita had reached the top job at his company, he still wanted to do more with electricity. So he designed an improved electrical socket and pitched it to his supervisors. Unfortunately, they didn't believe in its potential. Seeing no future with the company, Matsushita left and founded his own company. He named it Matsushita Electric Housewares Manufacturing Works, which would later become Panasonic.[1]

During the first few years, Matsushita ran every aspect of the company, including designing the products and doing most of the sales himself. But as his business took off, he could no longer handle running it on his own. He hired employees and spent less time on day-to-day operations. This gave him more time to think about the overall strategy to scale the company.

One of his primary insights was creating autonomous divisions within Panasonic. These divisions gave employees and managers more ownership over their business lines. As a result, Matsushita eliminated the layers of corporate bureaucracy that had held him back earlier in his career. Many other Japanese companies eventually copied Matsushita's corporate structure after hearing of its success. This earned Matsushita the nickname "the God of Management." At the time of his death in 1989, Panasonic was the largest consumer electronics company in the world.[2]

Kōnosuke Matsushita's story perfectly illustrates how we must shift our strategies to continue progressing in our careers. In other words, what we do for money at one point in time won't necessarily make sense at other points. For example, when I was in high school, I used to help my dad collect cans that we would recycle for the California state refund. At five cents a can, a few bags could easily fetch you forty to fifty dollars. Since then, my skills and earnings potential have increased significantly. Today, collecting cans isn't worth the time and effort anymore.

Matsushita had a similar revelation as he transitioned throughout his career. As he went from a job to starting his own company to scaling that company, he had to keep changing his strategy to get ahead. If he had stayed in his job as an inspector, he wouldn't have advanced much further than that. If he had never started delegating within his company, his business wouldn't have grown. Matsushita had to shift his focus throughout his career to continue progressing and earning more.

This same thinking also applies to how we should make career decisions as we climb the Wealth Ladder. While getting a second job or picking up extra shifts can make sense when you are lower on the Wealth Ladder, this will change as you climb it. In economics we call this an opportunity cost, or what you give up when you decide to do something. For example, if it takes me exactly five hours to write a blog post, my opportunity cost is anything else I could've done in that five hours. Alternatively, if it took me five hours to do a list of household chores, the opportunity cost of those chores would be writing one blog post.

Once you frame your career decisions in terms of their opportunity costs (i.e., what you give up), then you can determine whether a particular choice makes sense. Should you take that new job or stay where you are? Is that new investment worth your time? How about that side hustle you heard about? Once you know what you have to give up to take on a new job or side project, then you can decide if it's worth it. Unfortunately, this process is more difficult than it first appears, as highlighted in a blog post by Eric Jorgenson, writer and CEO at Scribe Media:

> As I reflect on my last year, the biggest mistakes I see are failures to change my decision-making to suit a new context. I form habits to pursue a specific goal in a specific context. As goals are accomplished, the context changes but the habit remains.[3]

Jorgenson realized that as he reached new heights in his professional life, he wasn't reevaluating his opportunity costs. He was still playing by old rules instead of adopting new ones. This would be like me still spending time collecting cans though I could make more money writing blog posts.

Thankfully, there is a cure for this problem—make sure to regularly reevaluate your opportunities costs. In other words, remember the phrase put forth by rapper Fat Joe, "Yesterday's price is not today's price." What you used to do for money may not be reflective of what you will do today for money. But how do we know when our opportunity costs have changed, and how does this relate to the Wealth Ladder?

When we discussed the intersection of spending and the Wealth Ladder in the previous chapter, we used the 0.01% Rule. This rule provided a decent guide for how we can spend money as we move up the Wealth Ladder. However, when it comes to *earning* money, the stakes need to be a bit higher. At Level 1 (<$10k), the 0.01% Rule would imply that you should make an earning decision based on whether it yields you an extra $1 (or less). That's far too small to make a difference in your financial life. Therefore, it needs to be a bit higher. How high is enough? 1 percent of your net worth.

If a particular income opportunity can increase your net worth by at least 1 percent, then you should do it. If not, then forget about it. We will call this the 1% Rule. The idea for the 1% Rule came from the same Eric Jorgenson blog post I just quoted. In that post, Jorgenson also discussed my Wealth Ladder framework and how you could apply it to your career.[4] Using the 1% Rule, here are some possible career options you should consider as you ascend the Wealth Ladder:

THE 1% RULE

- **LEVEL 1** (<$10k). Hourly jobs: $10–$100
- **LEVEL 2** ($10k–$100k). High-skilled work: $100–$1,000
- **LEVEL 3** ($100k–$1M). Career advancements; side hustles; small investments: $1,000–$10k
- **LEVEL 4** ($1M–$10M). Career pivots; start a business; medium investments: $10k–$100k
- **LEVEL 5** ($10M–$100M). Grow a business; large investments: $100k–$1M
- **LEVEL 6** ($100M+). Build an enterprise; significant investments: $1M+

As you can see, the types of income opportunities you will say no to will increase as you move up the Wealth Ladder. If you are in Level 1 you might be open to doing an odd job for fifty or a hundred dollars. But once you reach Level 2 (and above), you should focus on better earning opportunities.

The second thing you may notice as you move up the Wealth Ladder is that you spend less time working for money and more time having money work for you. This includes starting a business, where you employ others to help build your wealth, and investments, where you use your own money to do so. Let's briefly review how your earnings decisions change for each level of the Wealth Ladder.

In Level 1 (<$10k), you should be open to taking almost any income opportunity where you can earn extra money and build your skills. This includes getting a second job or doing gig work when it presents itself.

As you progress out of Level 1 and into Level 2 ($10k–

$100k), your focus should be on working smarter, rather than harder. While gig work and taking a second job can help get you out of Level 1, these tactics will be far less useful in helping you get out of Level 2. This is why Level 2 is about building up your skills so that you get paid more *per hour* going forward. Depending on what kind of work you do, there are a few different ways to improve your skills. You can enhance them on the job, through a paid educational program, or on your own time. Once you have such skills, then you should be able to get a job earning higher wages or charge people more when doing freelance work. This isn't the only way out of Level 2, but it's one that should work for most people.

Level 3 ($100k–$1M) is where career advancements, side hustles, and your individual investments can make a bigger difference in your income. At this stage, every decision you make should eventually add $1,000–$10,000 to your wealth. If you get a promotion or start a legitimate side hustle, you should see a jump in pay of around this size. As a result, you should be able to save even more money. For example, a great Level 1 to Level 2 strategy is tutoring to make extra income. However, to make this into a Level 3 strategy, you would need to expand it into a full-on side hustle. Advertising your services or hiring more tutors to work under your direction could make this happen.

Once you've reached Level 4 ($1M–$10M), the best way to increase your income is through career pivots, starting a business, and making additional investments. If you can pivot from one company to another where you will earn significantly more, you could easily see a pay increase exceeding $10,000 a year. More important, you don't have to wait until you are in Level 4 to go after these $10,000 (or larger) pay bumps. The only issue with this strategy is that you can't repeat it forever. There are only so many promotions you can get and career pivots you can make before your compensation starts to max out within an organization. In many industries, cash compensation has its upper limits.

If you hit this point, you may find yourself perpetually stuck in Level 4. Once here, it is highly unlikely that another raise or career pivot is going to get you to the next wealth level. This is why the most realistic way to continue to climb the Wealth Ladder beyond Level 4 is through business ownership. You have to start or join a business that earns you a lot of income or can be sold for a lot of income in the future. Even if you are very well paid (e.g., earning $500,000 a year), your job won't move the needle enough to get you out of Level 4. Run the numbers for yourself and you will see.

For example, imagine you earn $500,000 a year and can save $200,000 after you deduct income taxes and your cost of living. In this scenario, how long would it take you to reach Level 5 ($10M–$100M), assuming you just hit Level 4 ($1M–$10M)? If you earn 5 percent on your money, the answer is over twenty-one years. Yes, that's twenty-one years *after* you first became a millionaire while saving $200,000 annually and earning 5 percent a year. Even if you earned 10 percent annually, it would still take you nearly fifteen years to reach Level 5.

Therefore, if you want any chance of getting out of Level 4, you have to start or join a business that has significantly more upside than your career. While there are exceptions to this rule—for example, star athletes and entertainers—they are exceedingly rare. Most people in Level 5 have a significant portion of their wealth in a business or did so in the past. We will examine this further in the chapters that follow.

The same logic that holds for Level 4 is even more true once you are in Level 5 ($10M–$100M). The only way to progress when you have $10 million or more is by starting or scaling a business. This explains why Rihanna founded Fenty Beauty and George Clooney started and sold Casamigos. They both realized that there's more money to be made in business than in yet another song or movie. Other celebrities have since followed their lead.

However, you don't have to start a business to profit from it; you can join one and grow it as well. This is how Meg Whitman got rich with eBay and Howard Schultz with Starbucks. They didn't start these businesses, but they grew them in significant ways. Of course, growing a business is harder than it appears. It requires lots of work and at least a dose of luck to succeed.

Regardless of which earning strategy you choose to climb the Wealth Ladder, the data suggests that your income will be your primary tool to do so. If we look at the median U.S. household income in each wealth level, those higher on the Wealth Ladder earn more than those lower on the Wealth Ladder. As a reminder, the median is the middlemost value within a set of numbers. In this case, it represents the *typical* income for a household in a given Wealth Level. Here is a chart showing these median income values for U.S. households in 2022 by wealth level. These values come from the 2022 Survey of Consumer Finances, which is the latest data available with both income and wealth information.[5]

As you can see, the median household income in each wealth level is a bit higher than the one below it. Note that I excluded U.S. households in Level 6 from this chart because of how much they skew the *y*-axis. In particular, the median U.S. household income within each wealth level is shown in the following table.

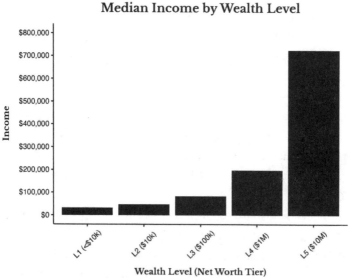

Median Income by Wealth Level

Source: Survey of Consumer Finances (2022)

Wealth Level	Median U.S. Household Income
Level 1 (<$10k)	$32,427
Level 2 ($10k–$100k)	$47,560
Level 3 ($100k–$1M)	$83,230
Level 4 ($1M–$10M)	$196,726
Level 5 ($10M–$100M)	$724,211
Level 6 ($100M+)	$4,266,359

This illustrates how much income and wealth tend to move together up the Wealth Ladder. It's rare to have high income with low wealth or high wealth with low income. In fact, if we were to break up U.S. households into four equal-size groups, or quartiles, based on their 2022 annual income, we would find that approximately:

- 25% earned less than $35k
- 25% earned $35k–$70k
- 25% earned $70k–$140k
- 25% earned more than $140k

These numbers aren't exact, but are approximated to be easy to remember. In this instance, the second group earns twice as much as the first ($70,000 = 2 * $35,000) and the third group earns twice as much as the second ($140,000 = 2 * $70,000).

They are also useful because these income groups are predictive of *current wealth*. The table on page 27 shows the 25th, 50th (median), and 75th percentile of wealth in 2022 for each of these four income groups. As a reminder, the 25th percentile is the point where 25 percent of households within a given group have a net worth below that value. The 50th percentile is the point where 50 percent of households within a given group have a net worth below that value. And so forth.

For example, 25 percent of the households in the lowest 25 percent of earners (i.e., those making less than $35,000 per year) have a net worth of less than $630. Half of households in the lowest 25 percent of earners have a net worth less than $18,360. Lastly, the top 25 percent of households in the lowest 25 percent of earners have a net worth *above* $135,900.

You can do the same exercise for each of the four income groups in the table.

Income Group	25th Percentile Wealth	50th Percentile Wealth	75th Percentile Wealth
Lowest 25% (<$35k)	$630	$18,360	$135,900
Second 25% ($35k–$70k)	$14,276	$88,170	$317,800
Third 25% ($70k–$140k)	$95,475	$236,400	$552,800
Highest 25% ($140k+)	$532,080	$1,217,700	$2,935,000

Ultimately, this data demonstrates that as income increases, so does wealth. This is one of the strongest relationships in all of personal finance. It's so strong that the *least wealthy* high earners have about four times more wealth than the *wealthiest* lowest earners. This illustrates a fundamental truth about getting rich—it all comes back to your income. Your income today is the foundation of your wealth tomorrow. It is the bedrock on top of which everything you desire financially will be built. To create this foundation, you'll need to follow some of the earning strategies outlined in this chapter. That could mean improving your skills, making investments, starting a business, or all of the above. There is no one-size-fits-all solution for increasing your income.

But here's the best part—you don't have to follow these strategies in order. The ideas proposed in each level of the Wealth Ladder are the *absolute minimum* you'd need to get to the next level. There's nothing that says you have to work multiple jobs, then get an education, then start your own business to move up. You can follow higher-level strategies even when you are lower on the Wealth Ladder!

However, these higher-level strategies tend to come with more risk than lower-level strategies. For example, starting a business is much harder than getting a 9-to-5 job. The job has a guaranteed payout and fixed working hours, while the business has neither. The job gives you money while the business requires your money to get it up and running. More importantly, the chance of massive success when starting a business is quite low. For every person that's sold a business for $10 million, there are many others that have failed to do so. In fact, about 25 percent of private businesses in the U.S. fail within the first year and 65 percent fail within the first ten years. These statistics have been relatively consistent for over three decades.[6] Level 5–6 strategies sound easy until you have to do them yourself.

For this reason, you can see why certain strategies on the Wealth Ladder may not work for everyone in every stage of their life. Some people are more suited to starting a business than others and some need more experience before they can go out on their own. This explains why it's easier to pursue higher-level strategies once you've already made some progress up the Wealth Ladder. This is exactly what Kōnosuke Matsushita did.

And you can do the same too. Once you have some money saved, you'll have more options at your disposal, and you can take bigger chances to earn more.

If you've ever played chess, you'll know this concept well. A certain move at a certain point in time may be foolish. But just a few turns later, that same move could shift the game in your favor. Ultimately, the move is only considered good or bad based on *when* it is played. The same is true when it comes to climbing the Wealth Ladder. A strategy that may be ill-advised for one person in one context could be perfect for another person in another context. The hard part is figuring out when to make such strategic transitions. This is what the Wealth Ladder is for.

As you climb it, you should see a dramatic shift in how you think about your career and your income. You'll go from working for money to having money work for you. This seemingly small shift in thinking can have a profound impact on how you spend your time and energy. For example, as you get to a certain point on the Wealth Ladder, you may stop prioritizing your traditional career altogether. Instead, you might start focusing on side projects and investments that offer more upside potential.

The framework to use when thinking about this problem is what Naval Ravikant calls leverage. And no, I'm not talking about the "borrowing money to invest" kind of leverage. I'm talking about the leverage that determines how much *output* you get for each unit of *input*. In this case the output is your future wealth, and the input is how you spend your time.

When Kim Kardashian promotes one of her products to her millions of followers, she will earn more from it than if you or I did the same thing. That's a form of leverage. As Ravikant explained, there are four kinds of leverage you can use to make more money: labor, capital, content, and code.[7] Each of these forms of leverage will allow you to divorce your time from your income, so that you can keep earning money without having to lift a finger. So let's review each of these types of leverage and where they fit on the Wealth Ladder.

Labor

The oldest and most ubiquitous form of leverage in human history is labor. Getting other people to help you build something is one of the most consistent ways to create long-term wealth. However, you need to ensure that what they create is more valuable than what you pay them. Also, since labor relies on the actions of other people, managing such relationships can be a challenge. Let's walk through an example to see why.

Imagine that you mow lawns for a living. It takes you thirty minutes (on average) to mow a lawn, and you charge $50 per lawn. In an eight-hour day, let's assume that you can mow twelve lawns, including travel time. This will generate $600 in revenue. Assume that your gear and gasoline costs roughly 15 percent of your sales. This means that your daily profit is around $510 (before taxes). But what happens if you employ someone to help you out for $20 an hour? Imagine that by doing so you can mow an additional six lawns in the same amount of time. So now you are mowing eighteen lawns a day at $50, for $900 in revenue. Netting out your gear costs of 15 percent, that leaves you with $765. However, you still have to pay your lawn care assistant their $160 daily wage ($20/hour * 8 hours). Netting that out, you have $605 in profit (before taxes). By employing another person, you went from $510 in daily profit to $605 in daily profit. You just generated an additional $95 in income for your lawn care business every single day.

This is a simplified example, but let's imagine scaling this business even further. You start hiring more people, buying more trucks with your logo on them, and working in more distant neighborhoods. Pretty soon your team is mowing a significant portion of the city's lawns. Eventually, running the business takes so much time that you stop mowing lawns altogether and focus on managing your employees instead. And guess what? Your earnings skyrocket. Since the cost of running the business and paying your employees is less than the revenue they generate, your earnings increase over time. The more employees you have and the more lawns they mow, the higher your profit, all else equal.

While the benefits of using labor as leverage are clear, this method of increasing your income isn't without its challenges. One of the primary downsides of using labor as leverage is that people can be difficult to work with. For example, what if one of your employees starts cutting corners (literally) to save time so that they can finish their work earlier in the day and go home? The quality of your service starts to suffer, and before you know it, you start losing customers. As you try to repair the reputational damage done by one employee, another crashes their lawn tractor into one of your client's homes. This causes $5,000 in damage. In the midst of this, a third employee complains about not getting paid enough and threatens to quit. Using labor as leverage is great when things go well, but it can cause all sorts of problems when they don't. This is why running a business that relies on other people can be incredibly difficult. However, if you can navigate this difficulty successfully, you will be rewarded for it.

While utilizing labor is a timeless method for growing your income, great leadership is needed to maximize its potential. Overall, labor as a form of leverage is a Level 3 ($100k–$1M) to Level 6 ($100M+) strategy, depending on how well it is managed and scaled.

LABOR SUMMARY

- **Pros:** Capitalizes on the difference between revenue generated and wages paid.

- **Cons:** Managing people can be challenging. Effective leadership and interpersonal skills are crucial for scaling and success.

Capital

The second-oldest form of leverage is using capital, or money, to increase your wealth. This can be done by using your own money to invest in a business or asset or by managing the wealth of others in exchange for a fee. The most popular use of capital as leverage is done by asset management firms (e.g., hedge funds, venture capitalists, etc.). These firms deploy other people's funds to generate a return that is (hopefully) better than what they could get elsewhere. These firms are incentivized to do this through a performance fee that gives them a share of the upside. Let's illustrate how this works using a hypothetical example.

Imagine you had the ability to beat the market (e.g., the S&P 500) by 10 percent every year no matter what. If the market was up 5 percent, you'd be up 15 percent. If the market went down 20 percent, you'd only lose 10 percent, and so on. Assuming you had $100,000 of your own money to invest, your market-beating ability would be worth $10,000 (10% * $100,000) in its first year. However, this would change dramatically if you had more capital.

Let's say that instead of using your own money, you decide to use other people's money to invest. You call up everyone you know and raise $1 million. Now, your 10 percent market-beating ability isn't worth $10,000, but $100,000. Unfortunately, you don't get to keep all of that $100,000, because some of that value has to go to the investors who gave you the $1 million in the first place. Assuming you charged your investors a 30 percent performance fee on all gains generated *above the market*, your market-beating skill would be worth around $30,000 a year. By using capital as leverage, you were able to increase the amount of income you earned from $10,000 to $30,000. That might not seem like a lot, but that's because you were only able to raise $1 million.

Imagine that after your first year all your clients tell their friends how good you are. Now those friends are beating down your door to invest with you. Before you know it, your fund has $10 million in it. Now your market-beating ability is worth $300,000 a year (ten times more than the prior year). This is simply because you have more capital at your disposal. You've leveraged your market-beating skills by 30x, from being worth $10,000 per year to $300,000 per year through capital alone.

Unfortunately, harnessing other people's money as a form of leverage has its challenges. Not only do people ask for their money back after a period of bad performance, but getting them to hand over their money in the first place is no easy task. The problem is that wealthy individuals receive pitches on what to do with their money all the time. With so many opportunities made available to them, it can be difficult to separate a worthwhile venture from a scam. In addition to the difficulty of raising capital, there can also be emotional challenges associated with investing other people's money. You might feel like you have a moral duty to protect them from loss, given that they trusted you with their life savings. This can be a heavy burden to bear as a money manager. Additionally, using capital can be risky if you fail to generate good returns. In such a scenario, your reputation as an asset manager could be permanently tarnished.

Whether you are a money manager or not, using capital as a form of leverage can carry significant financial risk. For example, if you borrow money to buy an investment property or start a business, you have no idea how it will turn out. You may be unable to rent out your investment property, or your business could fail. In either case, the only guarantee you will have is the payment due on your loan. If you find yourself in such a situation, you could end up losing lots of money or in bankruptcy. While capital is a great form of leverage on the upside, it can be destructive on the downside when things don't turn out as planned.

You don't have to borrow money to experience the downsides of using capital as leverage either. Simply investing your own funds into an asset that declines in value will do the trick. Watching your hard-earned money disappear before your eyes is a feeling that is unlike any other. As Fred Schwed Jr. wrote in *Where Are the Customers' Yachts?*, "Like all of life's rich emotional experiences, the full flavor of losing important money cannot be conveyed by literature."[8]

Using capital as a form of leverage can require managing financial risks in markets and emotional risks with people. Neither of these are easy tasks. Overall, using capital as a form of leverage is a Level 3 ($100k–$1M) to Level 6 ($100M+) strategy, depending on the amount of capital that is utilized and how successful you are at deploying it.

CAPITAL SUMMARY

- **Pros:** You can build wealth more quickly by using other people's money.

- **Cons:** Demands a specific skill set, especially in sales and emotional regulation. Heightened financial risk.

Content

In 1440, Johannes Gutenberg invented the printing press and changed the world forever. Before then, content had to be produced by hand, typically one copy at a time. After Gutenberg, content could be produced at scale. With time, the price of content production continued to decrease, and, once the internet was invented, it essentially went to zero. Today, you can produce content once and share it as many times as you want. Jack Butcher famously branded this idea as "build once, sell twice."[9] For this reason, content creation can be considered the ultimate form of leverage.

And in the internet age, content and media are permissionless. I don't have to ask for anyone's permission to share my work (assuming it is legal). With other forms of leverage, this isn't the case. You need permission to utilize someone's labor or capital. You have to pay them for their time or their money. But this isn't true with content. While any social media company could ban me from sharing my content, I have other options. There is nothing stopping me from posting on my website or writing books indefinitely. The same is true for you or anyone else.

The good news is that it's never been easier to share content at scale. Unfortunately, that's the bad news as well. Because the barriers to create and share content are so low, anyone can do it. And since the competition is so fierce, it can be incredibly difficult to stand out and build an audience. When there are thousands of people doing the same thing as you, you have to create top-tier, *differentiated* content to get noticed.

Lastly, the popularity of content is generally short-lived. Something that goes viral today is unlikely to be shared more in the future. This is why creating content can be such a grind. You spend a lot of time putting work into something that quickly fades into the background. The only exception to this rule is content that is high quality and evergreen. Unfortunately, creating such content takes a tremendous amount of effort and a bit of luck as well.

In full, content is an incredible form of leverage, but requires excellence and consistency to stand out. Additionally, unlike the other forms of leverage we've seen thus far, content is generally only a Level 2 ($10k–$100k) to Level 4 ($1M–$10M) strategy. While you can make good money from content, to get to Level 5 ($10M–$100M) or higher, you typically need to have another form of leverage at your disposal. For example, many ultrasuccessful content creators also have their own businesses, which employ a team of people to sell higher-value products such as cohort-based courses, high-end coaching, or exclusive online communities. In each of these cases, the content is the marketing engine to scale the business. In other words, one form of leverage (content) is helping to build another (labor).

CONTENT SUMMARY

- **Pros:** Incredibly scalable. Low barrier to entry. Little or no permission needed.
- **Cons:** Lots of competition. Difficult to build an audience.

Content is generally short-lived unless it is high quality and evergreen.

Code

In today's digital age, code grants you the ability to create immense leverage using just lines of text as instruction. Think about the websites you visit or the apps you rely on daily. All of them were built once and then replicated millions (or billions) of times for others to use.

For example, consider someone creating a mobile game. They might spend months or years developing it, but once it's released their work is done. If they sell the app for $9.99 and ten thousand people download it, that's nearly $100,000 in gross revenue (before fees). That's $100,000 that was created with no extra work on their part. This is the power of code as leverage.

In addition, like content and media, this form of leverage is permissionless. I don't have to ask anyone for permission to write code and share it on the internet. I can do it 100 percent on my own. Of course, if you were to sell an app through a platform, such as Apple's App Store, you would need permission from Apple to do so. Nevertheless, the permission needed to share code is low compared to other forms of leverage.

Despite its many benefits, as a form of leverage code has its own unique challenges. Coding requires high technical skill. This means domain knowledge and keeping up with the ever-evolving tech landscape. You have to enjoy continuous learning if you want to code for the long haul. While the rise of AI and other large language models (LLMs) like ChatGPT have made coding much easier, you will still need some familiarity with programming to use these tools effectively.

In addition, coding requires ongoing maintenance of your code. Systems change and things break. Though I said that the "work is done" once an app is released, this is rarely the case. You'll have to fix bugs and maintain your code to ensure that it works over time and as systems evolve. This can be a challenge all its own.

Lastly, the digital space is quite crowded. With thousands of new apps and websites launched daily, you will need to be able to market your work for it to reach the necessary scale to stand out. Being a great programmer is one thing, but turning that into a moneymaking app is another.

Nevertheless, code remains an attractive form of leverage in today's technological landscape. This is true despite the high skills that are typically required. On the Wealth Ladder, code is a Level 3 ($100k–$1M) to Level 5 ($10M–$100M) strategy, depending on how you monetize your skills. Historically, learning to program was the ticket to a six-figure salary, which could easily get someone into Level 3 or Level 4 of the Wealth Ladder. But getting to Level 5 (and beyond) with code requires a bit more. This usually means joining a start-up early, where you get significant equity, or using code and labor to create a valuable business.

CODE SUMMARY

- **Pros:** Near infinite scalability. Little or no permission needed.
- **Cons:** Technical skills are required, as is ongoing maintenance of the code in case of bugs and system updates. Effective marketing is essential to achieve significant scale.

Now that we have reviewed the four kinds of leverage, here is a summary table to illustrate where each fits on the Wealth Ladder.

Form of Leverage	Pros	Cons	Wealth Ladder Level
Labor	Allows for higher income generation by capitalizing on the difference between revenue generated and wages paid.	Managing people can be challenging. Effective leadership and interpersonal skills are crucial for scaling and success.	Levels 3–6
Capital	You can build wealth more quickly by using other people's money.	Demands a specific skill set, especially in sales and emotional regulation. Heightened financial risk.	Levels 3–6
Content	Incredibly scalable. Low barrier to entry. Little or no permission needed.	Lots of competition. Difficult to build an audience. Content is generally short-lived unless it is high quality and evergreen.	Levels 2–4
Code	It has near infinite scalability and requires little or no permission.	Technical skills are required, as is ongoing maintenance of the code in case of bugs and system updates. Effective marketing is essential to achieve significant scale.	Levels 3–5

Chapter 2 Summary

- What you do for money should change as you get more of it.

- Income creates wealth. This is the strongest relationship in personal finance. It's rare to have high income with low wealth or high wealth with low income.

- Your income today is the foundation of your wealth tomorrow.

- To raise your income, build skills and increase your leverage.

When it comes to your earnings decisions as you climb the Wealth Ladder, you have many options at your disposal. For some, that will mean getting promoted at their current employer. For others, it will require going out on their own and starting a business. Kōnosuke Matsushita did both, but only when the timing was right for him. You should do the same. After all, there is no hard rule that says what you should or shouldn't do based on your wealth level. Rather, you should find the strategy that works for you.

Whatever you decide to do, some form of leverage will be necessary if you want to continue climbing the Wealth Ladder. And for some of us, the best form of leverage is how we invest *our own* money. For this, we turn to our next chapter.

CHAPTER 3

Investing up
the Wealth Ladder

B etween March 23, 2020, and November 4, 2021, Elon Musk's net worth increased from $25 billion to $340 billion as Tesla's stock price soared. Over this twenty-month period, Musk's wealth grew by, on average, over $1 billion every two days, or $6,000 per second. The increase in Musk's wealth *in a single week* would've qualified for the Forbes 400 list on its own. Every time Musk went to sleep he woke up over $100 million richer. To put this in perspective, in the time it's taken you to read this paragraph Musk's net worth would've increased by over $100,000.

Musk's ballooning fortune during this period was the fastest accumulation of wealth in human history. No one had ever seen such a rapid increase in their resources in such a short period of time. But Musk's colossal growth in wealth was not completely by chance. It had a lot to do with how he invested his money. Like many of those in Level 6 ($100M+), Musk doesn't have the bulk of his assets in his cars, his homes, or his retirement accounts. No, people in Level 6 invest most of their wealth in businesses, which they tend to have control of. Because of this, they can see their fortunes rise (and fall) in quick fashion.

But how do the rest of those on the Wealth Ladder tend to invest? Based on the 2022 Survey of Consumer Finances, we can examine how wealth is broken out for the six levels of the Wealth Ladder among U.S. households.[1] In particular, we will summarize the percentage of total assets held in each of the follow asset categories:

- Cash
- Vehicles
- Primary residence
- Retirement
- Real estate (outside of primary residence)
- Mutual funds/stocks
- Business interests

This will give us a much better idea of how households tend to invest across the Wealth Ladder, which will help inform your own investment decisions.

To begin, let's look at the percentage of total assets of U.S. households held in cash versus other assets, for each of the six levels of the Wealth Ladder. As you'll see in the chart on the following page, cash makes up nearly 40 percent of the assets for those in Level 1, but 10 percent (or less) for those in the other Wealth Levels.

This major difference in cash holdings is likely because

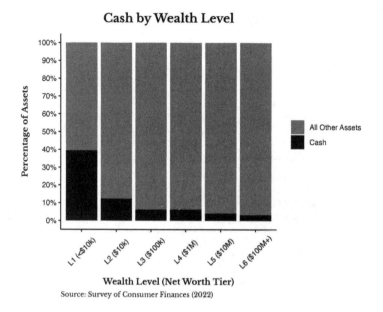

Cash by Wealth Level

Wealth Level (Net Worth Tier)
Source: Survey of Consumer Finances (2022)

Level 1 households don't tend to own many assets outside of cash. In fact, the only asset class that U.S. households in Level 1 own more of than cash is vehicles.

We can see this in the plot on the following page, which illustrates how each wealth level has less vehicle wealth than the level below it. This pattern is similar to what we saw when we looked at cash holdings by wealth level. The primary difference between cash and vehicle wealth is that U.S. households in Level 2 ($10k–$100k) have significantly more of their assets in vehicles than in cash.

For those in Level 1, vehicles and cash make up nearly 85 percent of their total assets. But for those in Level 2, vehicles and cash make up only about 50 percent of their total assets.

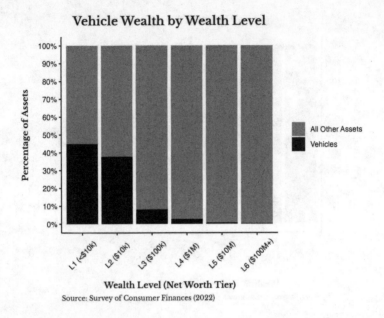

Vehicle Wealth by Wealth Level

Source: Survey of Consumer Finances (2022)

What makes up the rest of the assets for those households in Level 2? Mostly their primary residence.

When we subset to U.S. households that actually own their own home, we see that the percentage of total assets in a primary residence is quite high. For example, as shown on the following page, among homeowners in Levels 1–3, between 65 percent and 75 percent of their total assets are in their primary residence.

From this chart alone we can see why homeownership is so touted in the United States. For many U.S. households, it comprises a large fraction of their wealth. Homeownership is central to the American Dream and it's also the primary way in which U.S. households transfer wealth to the next generation.

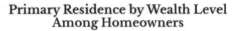

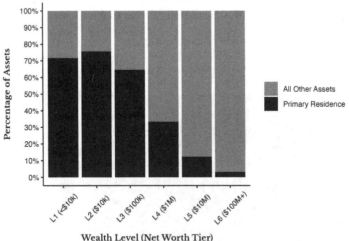

Primary Residence by Wealth Level Among Homeowners

Wealth Level (Net Worth Tier)

Source: Survey of Consumer Finances (2022)

So far, we've reviewed the main asset classes for those in Levels 1–3—cash, vehicles, and a primary residence. But what is different about the households in Levels 4–6? What do they tend to hold more of that those in Levels 1–3 hold less of? The answer is income-producing assets. Income-producing assets are assets that you expect to generate income for you far into the future. This can include stocks, bonds, real estate, and your own private business. The exact percentages of each of these asset classes varies across Levels 4–6. Nevertheless, the important thing to keep in mind is the shift that takes place toward income-producing assets as you go from Levels 1–3 to Levels 4–6. This becomes even more evident when we examine the data.

45

For example, if we look at the percentage of total assets in retirement accounts, we see that U.S. households in Level 4 ($1M–$10M) hold the most on a relative basis.

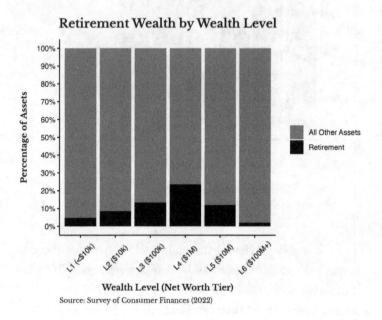

Retirement Wealth by Wealth Level

Source: Survey of Consumer Finances (2022)

We also know that retirement accounts tend to hold income-producing assets such as stocks and bonds. This highlights the shift toward income-producing assets that occurs for those higher on the Wealth Ladder. Don't get me wrong, those in Levels 1–3 have money in retirement accounts as well, but they tend to own more non-income-producing assets, including the ones we've reviewed so far (e.g., cash, vehicles, primary residence).

But it's not just retirement accounts where we see this divergence in ownership between those in Levels 1–3 and those in
Levels 4–6. We see it in real estate and stock ownership too. If
we look at the amount of real estate owned *outside* of the primary residence, we see that those in Levels 4–6 hold the highest
percentage relative to their total assets.

Real Estate by Wealth Level

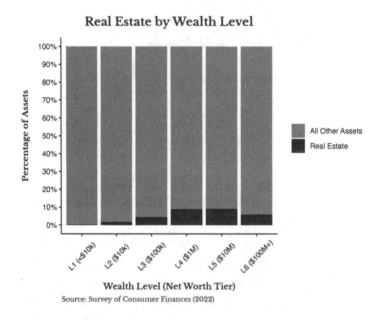

Wealth Level (Net Worth Tier)
Source: Survey of Consumer Finances (2022)

The same thing is true of stock ownership by wealth level.
When we compare the percentage of total assets in stocks and
mutual funds (excluding retirement accounts) across the Wealth
Ladder, the divergence is striking.

Once again, we see a night-and-day difference between how
those in Levels 4–6 and those in Levels 1–3 invest their money.

Stocks and Mutual Funds by Wealth Level

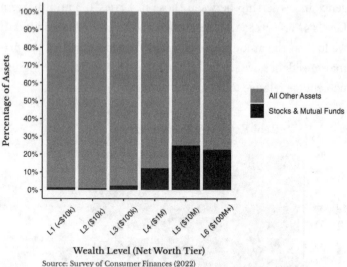

Wealth Level (Net Worth Tier)
Source: Survey of Consumer Finances (2022)

Those in Levels 4–6 have anywhere from 12 percent to 25 percent of their wealth in stocks outside of retirement accounts, while those in Levels 1–3 have less than 3 percent of their wealth allocated in the same way. More importantly, stocks and mutual funds represent the largest asset class for those in Level 5 and the second-largest asset class for those in Level 6.

But what separates those households in Level 6 from everyone else? What is their largest asset holding? Business interests, or the ownership of businesses where there is some personal involvement (e.g., founder, partner, etc.). When we look at the percentage of total assets allocated to business interests by wealth level, we can see that this is where Level 6 stands out.

This is how individuals like Elon Musk, Bill Gates, and others are able to generate so much wealth (at least on paper). They own

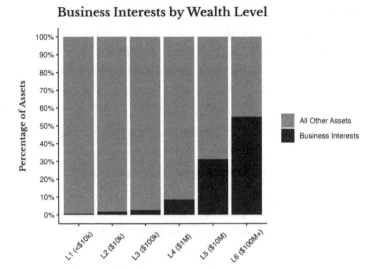

Business Interests by Wealth Level

Wealth Level (Net Worth Tier)

Source: Survey of Consumer Finances (2022)

a significant share of a business, or set of businesses, that become incredibly valuable over time. Outside of highly paid entertainers, lottery winners, and heirs to large inheritances, most people in Level 5 and Level 6 got wealthy through business ownership. Whether they start a company or acquire a significant part of its equity over time, this is their typical strategy.

Such a strategy has its pros and cons. On one hand, it's great to have your own business because it can generate so much wealth for you. On the other hand, if your business runs into trouble, you can see your fortune decline rather quickly. This is the key trade-off associated with this higher-level strategy.

Now that we've examined how people invest across the Wealth Ladder, let's summarize the most commonly held asset classes within each wealth level:

- **LEVEL 1** (<$10k): Cash and vehicles
- **LEVEL 2** ($10k–$100k): Vehicles and primary residence
- **LEVEL 3** ($100k–$1M): Primary residence and retirement accounts
- **LEVEL 4** ($1M–$10M): Primary residence, retirement accounts, stocks
- **LEVEL 5** ($10M–$100M): Business interests, stocks, retirement accounts
- **LEVEL 6** ($100M+): Business interests and stocks

From this data we can see a general pattern for how wealth accumulation tends to occur across wealth levels:

Cash/Vehicles → Home/Retirement → Stocks/Business Ownership

Those with fewer assets tend to own the things they need to survive (e.g., cash, vehicles, a home). But as individuals gain more wealth, they tend to invest in assets that generate even more wealth for themselves (e.g., stocks, bonds, businesses, etc.).

You may see this and think, "If those in Levels 5–6 tend to own their own businesses, why should I bother investing in anything else? Why not just go all-in on being a business owner?" Well, because business ownership *by itself* does not guarantee that you will make it to Levels 5–6. Though most people in Levels 5–6 own businesses, that does not mean that every business owner makes it to Levels 5–6. This would be like me interviewing a bunch of lottery winners and discovering that they all bought lottery tickets every single week. Does this imply that buying lottery tickets every week is a good financial strategy? Obviously not.

Unfortunately, ownership doesn't guarantee results. In other words, starting a business won't turn you into Bill Gates any more than buying stocks will turn you into Warren Buffett. However, the correlation between how individuals invest and their level on the Wealth Ladder is quite strong. As we saw in the diagram above, as people move up the Wealth Ladder their assets tend to shift from things that *cost* them money to things that *make* them money. In other words, they move away from non-income-producing assets toward income-producing assets. When we plot the percentage of assets that are income producing by wealth level, this relationship is undeniable.

It's more income-producing assets all the way up the Wealth Ladder. This distinction is particularly prominent when

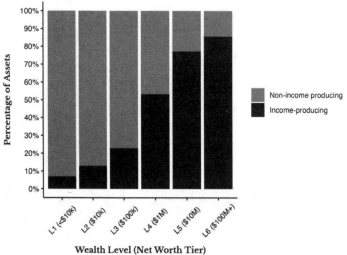

Income-Producing Assets by Wealth Level

Wealth Level (Net Worth Tier)
Source: Survey of Consumer Finances (2022)

we compare those in Levels 1–3 to those in Levels 4–6. In general, those in Levels 1–3 have 20 percent or less of their total assets as income-producing assets. But those in Levels 4–6 have 50 percent or *more* of their total assets as income-producing assets. If I had to pick a single investment idea that separates these two groups on the Wealth Ladder, this would be it. This explains why the mantra of my first book, *Just Keep Buying*, was: "The continual purchase of a diverse set of income-producing assets."[2]

This is the approach I stand by for most people trying to move up the Wealth Ladder. Of course, there's more to financial success than how you invest your money. But if you want to emulate the wealthiest investors, owning more income-producing assets is a good place to start.

Chapter 3 Summary

- Households lower on the Wealth Ladder tend to have most of their wealth in cash, vehicles, and their primary residence.

- Households higher on the Wealth Ladder tend to have most of their wealth in retirement accounts, stocks, real estate, and private businesses.

- Ownership doesn't guarantee results. Starting a business won't turn you into Bill Gates any more than buying stocks will turn you into Warren Buffett.

- In general, households in Levels 1–3 own assets that cost them money, while those in Levels 4–6 own assets that make them money.

- As households ascend the Wealth Ladder they tend to own a larger share of income-producing assets.

Now that we've looked at spending, income, and investing across the Wealth Ladder, let's turn our attention to each of its individual levels. What is it like to be in each level? How do you get to higher levels? And, most important, what can you do to prevent yourself from falling down the Wealth Ladder?

PART II

MAKING

THE

CLIMB

A Note on Part II

I've written Part II with the aim of helping you on your wealth-building journey *based on where you are today*. You can go right to the chapter on your current wealth level, but I recommend reading the chapters in order. This will provide a bigger-picture understanding of the Wealth Ladder, and will highlight the wealth-building strategies that could be helpful to the other people in your life. We all have friends, family, and coworkers across the Wealth Ladder who could benefit from such strategies.

Nevertheless, if a particular chapter or section isn't relevant to you, feel free to skip ahead. Trust me, I won't mind. I'd rather you focus on what is most useful to you today than stop reading altogether. For reference, I've included the page numbers that start the chapter for each individual wealth level:

- Chapter 4: Level 1 (<$10k): page 59
- Chapter 5: Level 2 ($10k–$100k): page 71
- Chapter 6: Level 3 ($100k–$1M): page 85
- Chapter 7: Level 4 ($1M–$10M): page 99
- Chapter 8: Level 5 ($10M–$100M): page 113
- Chapter 9: Level 6 ($100M+): page 133

Level 1 (<$10k)

―――――

Atypical Results Require Atypical Actions

magine you had to start your financial life over. Your bank account goes to zero. You cut off all your connections. Your résumé is wiped clean. This is what Mike Black did in 2020 near the beginning of the COVID-19 pandemic. At the time, he was the founder of a successful software development company. However, Mike wanted to show that it was possible to go from $0 to $1 million in earnings within twelve months. So he began filming a reality series about his experiment. He called it the Million Dollar Comeback.

To start, Mike gave up everything he had. He cut off his connections, started with no money in a new bank account, and assumed a new identity. Overnight he went from a successful entrepreneur to a vagrant wandering the streets of Austin, Texas. His only belongings were a backpack, a cell phone with internet, and a single change of clothes.

On the first day of his experiment, Mike looked for a place to stay so that he could find a way to make money. He lucked out his first night, when a complete stranger offered to let him crash in his RV after Mike contacted him through the internet. Mike now had a place to stay, but still didn't have any cash. And without any form of transportation, many of the jobs Mike looked at were out of reach.

So Mike came up with a clever idea to make money. He would take free furniture from Craigslist and sell it on Facebook Marketplace. But the real genius behind his plan was that he didn't have to pick up the furniture. He became the middleman, and took a piece of the profit. Within two days, Mike had $300 in his bank account. With this money, he was able to get more clothing, a computer, and rent a coworking space for only $40 a month. This allowed him to get started on an e-commerce business.

Nevertheless, by the end of the month, Mike had a problem. He only had $4 to his name, yet still had to pay the rent for the RV and his cell phone bill for the month. With the financial cliff approaching, Mike applied for ten jobs and got one as a virtual assistant making $25 an hour. This gave him the lifeline he needed to stay afloat and get his ecommerce business off the ground. Shortly thereafter, he secured some retainer agreements with his clients to get more consistent revenue. This stabilized his business income and allowed him to keep growing.

Things were going well for Mike until he received devastating personal news. His father had been diagnosed with stage 4 colon cancer and was given twelve months to live. Mike debated whether to end the experiment early, but decided to keep going in honor of his dad. Though he was in a difficult place emotionally, Mike continued scaling his e-commerce business. He ran Facebook ads and focused on getting customers to buy recurring subscriptions. His plan worked. By the tenth month of the experiment, Mike's business was making nearly $10,000 in recurring monthly revenue.

That's when he revealed the biggest surprise of the experiment yet—he had to end it early. During the course of filming, Mike had been diagnosed with two autoimmune diseases. Due to the toll they were taking on his body, he decided to stop the experiment and focus on his health. Mike earned $65,000 in ten months, far less than his original goal of $1 million. Despite failing to reach his objective, he inspired many through a YouTube series he created about the experience.[1]

—

The story of Mike Black and his Million Dollar Comeback highlights a lot of what it's like to be in Level 1 of the Wealth Ladder. There's the uncertainty and stress around not having money. There's the difficulty of finding opportunities even when you are willing to work. And last, there's the major setback you can experience if you have health problems. As William T. Vollmann stated in *Poor People*, "Poverty is wretched subnormality of opportunity and circumstances."[2] This is exactly what Mike experienced on his journey from zero dollars to $1 million—difficult circumstances and lack of opportunity. Despite his high motivation, Mike had to overcome many obstacles to make money. And he did this while having many more advantages than others. He had an education, valuable skills, and a nice life to fall back on in case he failed. Imagine how hard it would be for someone in a similar situation *without* such advantages?

This is the reality if you're in Level 1. Your opportunities are limited and you are overly exposed to the impact of bad luck. One thing goes wrong, and your life could go into a tailspin. If you get injured, you could lose your job. If you lose your job, you could go into debt. So on and so forth. A typical inconvenience for someone higher on the Wealth Ladder can be a crisis for someone in Level 1. This is because bad luck is amplified in Level 1, and this amplification can lead to people getting into a financial hole they can't escape from. This explains why less than 10 percent of people account for over half of the financial distress events in the United States.[3] Once you fall into such a cycle, it can be very hard to get out.

What's even more unfortunate is that you can fall behind through no fault of your own. Mike Black had to end his experiment early due to health problems. This explains why 44 percent of those who filed for personal bankruptcy in the U.S. "very much" or "somewhat" agreed that illness-related job loss was a factor.[4] If you get so sick that you can no longer work, it's incredibly difficult to stay afloat financially. Unfortunately, you can't necessarily prevent a negative health outcome. While diet and exercise may help, there are no guarantees when it comes to your health.

Putting negative health outcomes aside, the other thing you need to avoid in Level 1 is a crippling level of debt. Whether it's credit cards or excessive student loans, debt can be the anchor in your financial life that prevents you from moving forward. As Warren Buffett once said, "If you start revolving debt on credit cards, you are going to be paying 18 or 20 percent. You can't make progress in your financial life going around borrowing money at 18 or 20 percent."[5] If one of the greatest investors of all time couldn't make money borrowing at such high rates, you won't either. This is why it is imperative to get your debt levels under control before you can start to make your way out of Level 1.

We see this clearly in the data as well. When we look at total debt over net worth for U.S. households by wealth level, we see that households in Level 1 tend to have much higher *average* debt levels than everyone else.[6]

The average debt over net worth for those in Level 1 exceeds 300 percent. Note that this is *after* I subset to households with a net worth exceeding $1,000. Without such a filter, the average debt over net worth for households in Level 1 would be even higher. Unfortunately, a small number of heavily indebted households bias this average upward even with the $1,000 net worth filter.

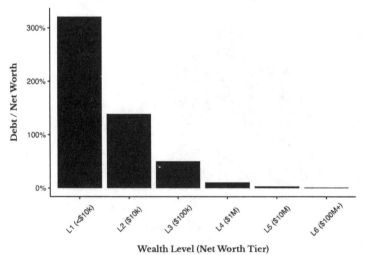

Average Debt over Net Worth by Wealth Level

Source: Survey of Consumer Finances (2022)
Note: Households with a net worth less than $1,000 have been excluded.

We can adjust for this by showing the median debt over net worth by wealth level instead. In this instance, the median represents the *typical* debt level (relative to net worth) for households within a given wealth level. As you can see below, when we use median debt over net worth things don't look as bad.

Compared to the average, the median debt over net worth isn't highest in Level 1, but Level 2. This suggests that having debt isn't necessarily a problem, but having lots of it can be. In other words, you don't have to get completely out of debt to exit Level 1. But if you find yourself in a financial hole, stop digging. This might require extreme action on your part including: cutting your spending, working multiple jobs, and more. I am generally not a fan of such drastic behaviors, as I will dis-

Median Debt over Net Worth by Wealth Level

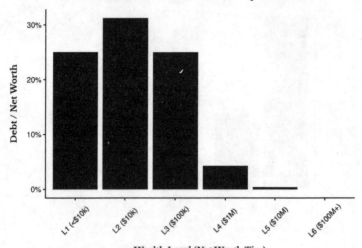

Source: Survey of Consumer Finances (2022)
Note: Households with a net worth less than $1,000 have been excluded.

cuss in a moment. However, in difficult situations they can be warranted. Atypical results require atypical actions. And if you are in crippling debt, then you may need to go above and beyond to exit Level 1 and get back on track.

If you find yourself in such a situation, it's okay. You just need to get moving in the right direction. Before you do anything though, get in the right headspace. Beating yourself up over your previous financial mistakes won't do you any good. Unfortunately, sulking and self-hatred won't help you pay down your debt any faster.

Instead, you should examine how you spend your time and money. Do you have free time in your week to earn extra income? What about time to learn a new skill? Is there anything you could easily stop spending money on? If you can identify areas where you can make progress like this, work on them. The goal is to reduce how much monthly debt you add, and eventually to start reducing your debt altogether. This process won't be easy, but you have to do it if you want a less stressful financial life.

While taking atypical actions can help, the best way out of Level 1 is not to fall behind in the first place. And to avoid falling behind, you need to build a buffer against bad luck. Since bad luck is amplified in Level 1, your goal should be to reduce its impact. This means setting aside cash for emergencies, or saving money. However, the most common advice many financial experts give to save money is to "cut your spending." Unfortunately, this advice is mostly useless to most people in Level 1. Not only is the advice not novel (who hasn't heard of spending less?), but the data suggests there isn't much spending to cut anyway. What little money people have in Level 1 is usually spent on the necessities (e.g., rent, food, etc.). This explains why in 2020 the lowest 20 percent of income earners in the U.S. spent over 100 percent of their after-tax income on the necessities. Housing, food, transportation, and health care consumed their whole paycheck and then some.[7] To survive, you usually take out debt or get assistance from family members. For many in Level 1, cutting spending isn't the ideal solution, because there just isn't room to cut.

This is why the real problem in Level 1 isn't spending, it's income. If you want to make it out of Level 1, you have to raise your income so that you can save money. Of course, this isn't easy, but it's the only sustainable way out of Level 1 and up the Wealth Ladder. While there are many ways to raise your income, the one I want you to focus on in Level 1 is building marketable skills. In other words, get good at things that people will pay you for. But I want you to do this *without* spending much money. Ideally, you won't need to take out lots of debt to build marketable skills and raise your income. Below are a few ways you can go about doing this.

First, get any job you can and work incredibly hard at it. If you work hard at a job, you will stand out against your peers and be given opportunities to learn more. I've read countless stories of people who escaped poverty by going above and beyond in a low-paying job. While their peers complained or did the bare minimum, they grinded it out and got noticed. They did whatever was asked of them and kept showing up. As a result, they got more chances to expand their skill set and earn more.

Of course, hard work isn't foolproof. If you find yourself in a situation where your hard work isn't being noticed, then you should find another opportunity. Some signs of being in this situation include: being in the same role for years without a promotion, lack of feedback or praise from your supervisors, and not being given more responsibility. While working hard won't succeed 100 percent of the time, if you are starting out, it's not a bad way to go.

Another way to build marketable skills on the cheap is to offer to help someone out for free. While these opportunities won't make you any money immediately, if they give you valuable experience, they can be worth the effort. Offering to help for free is basically the same as paying for training. But instead of paying with your money, you pay with your time. While such an arrangement could be exhausting if you have a full-time job, it could also change the trajectory of your career.

Lastly, a third way to build marketable skills is to get an education. The right education can increase your chances of landing a higher-paying role. Unfortunately, the downside of getting an education is that it typically costs money. And if you are struggling in Level 1, taking on lots of debt probably isn't the right move. This is why those in Level 1 should focus on getting an education for as cheaply as possible. Either find low-cost resources to learn from or only consider borrowing if a high payoff seems likely. The last thing someone in Level 1 should do is borrow a lot of money for a worthless piece of paper.

Of course, I am a huge proponent of education, but not all education is created equal. This explains why more than half of all millennial college graduates regretted what they studied or how much they paid for it.[8] If they could go back, they likely would make different choices. Some of them would've picked a major that would have enabled them to earn more after graduation. Others would've chosen a cheaper school, so they didn't have to take out student loans. This is why I consider paying for an education to be more of a Level 2 strategy. Because taking out student loans without earning more is a recipe for getting trapped in Level 1. On the other hand, if you're in Level 2, you can take these kinds of risks and be okay if they don't work out. We will discuss the importance of education in more detail in the next chapter. For now, if you're in Level 1 and want to get an education, don't overpay for it.

No matter which strategy you choose to build marketable skills, this is a *long-term* solution to getting out of Level 1. Raising your income takes time. It won't happen overnight. However, if you need a quicker fix, then you should utilize the wealth that you already have. I'm not talking about the wealth in your bank account. I'm talking about your relationships.

As Ruby K. Payne stated in *A Framework for Understanding Poverty*, "In poverty, people are possessions, and people rely on each other in order to survive. . . . After all, that is all you have— people."[9] So if you find yourself in a tough spot financially, find the people in your life who can help out. Poverty can be a scary thing, so don't be afraid to rely on friends or family to support you as you get your financial life together.

Note that if you do follow such a strategy, be ready to pay back the favor at some point in the future. When researchers analyzed the borrowing and lending activity of the poorest households, they found that "almost every household borrowed informally from family and friends, and many, including the very poor, reciprocated by offering such loans to others."[10] This is the social contract that is common throughout the world. Ask for help when you need it, but be ready to help when called upon. While this may slow your progress up the Wealth Ladder, it's also one way to get started up it yourself.

Relying on your relationships is the kind of financial advice that often gets overlooked. Unfortunately, relationships aren't as easy to measure as money in your bank account. Chris Arnade echoed this sentiment in his book *Dignity*: "We primarily valued what we could measure, and that meant material wealth. The things that couldn't be easily measured—community, dignity, faith, happiness—were largely ignored because they were hard to see—especially from so far away."[11] While those lower on the Wealth Ladder may have fewer zeros in their net worth, these same households have far more wealth than meets the eye. Finding ways to utilize this wealth is how you can escape Level 1.

Overall, life in Level 1 can be challenging. Even when you know how to get out, unforeseen events can still get in the way. This is what happened to Mike Black when he failed to earn $1 million a year after starting from zero. His experiment demonstrated the true difficulty of starting with nothing, even when you have skills and a good education. But what Black's experiment didn't account for is the wealth of relationships that many in Level 1 do have access to. After all, humans wouldn't be where we are today without helping one another out. So if you find yourself struggling in Level 1, use this to your advantage and ask others for assistance. Then, once you are out of Level 1, you can provide the same help to others who need it.

> ## Level 1 Summary
>
> - **Follow-Up:** Examine how you spend your time and money. Reduce debt and build an emergency fund.
>
> - **Opportunities:** Focus on building marketable skills without spending money. Rely on family and friends where possible.
>
> - **Risks:** Credit card debt, student loans (without the expectation of higher income), and other big financial liabilities.
>
> - **Mental framework:** Atypical results require atypical actions.

—

Now that we have an idea of what things are like in Level 1, let's look at Level 2 and why your career decisions are of the utmost importance here.

CHAPTER 5

Level 2 ($10k–$100k)

Learn Today, Earn Forever

ászló Polgár had a bold theory. He believed that any human could be turned into a genius if given intense training from an early age. His belief was rooted in research he had done on some of history's greatest thinkers. After studying their lives, Polgár realized that they all shared two things in common. First, they spent countless hours learning their craft. No matter what they were studying, they practiced far more than their peers. Second, they started at a very young age. Based on his findings, Polgár concluded that genius was made, not born.

But that wasn't enough for the Hungarian educational psychologist. Polgár wanted to prove his theory without question. So he told a foreign-language teacher named Klara of his idea and they agreed to marry and have children to test it out. The two had three daughters, all of whom Polgár trained to play chess. Though they considered other fields of study for their daughters, they chose chess because it was "very objective and easy to measure."[1]

Decades after the Polgárs started their experiment, it became clear that it was a massive success. All three of their daughters grew into world-class chess players. Two of them became grandmasters, the highest title awarded in chess. And their youngest daughter, Judit, is considered the greatest female chess player of all time and the only woman ever to rank in the top ten worldwide.

László Polgár's radical experiment demonstrates the impact that education can have on lifetime achievement. And though you probably aren't trying to become a chess prodigy, his ideas are just as applicable to your career. This is especially true if you're in Level 2 of the Wealth Ladder, because this is where education can have the biggest impact on your future wealth. While education is important no matter where you are on the Wealth Ladder, in Level 2 you have a unique opportunity to capitalize on it. Why? Because this is the level where you have enough money to afford it, but not so much money that it's not worth the effort.

For example, imagine someone in Level 1 who takes out a student loan to get a degree. If that degree boosts their income, the loan can be worth it. However, if it doesn't, their student debt could set them further back than where they started. Now consider someone who's already accumulated quite a bit of wealth in Level 4 or higher. Do you think it makes *financial* sense for them to stop what they're doing to get a degree? I'm not so sure. Not only might they have to give up their income while getting their degree, but they'd also have to pay for it. So unless that degree can drastically increase their income, it probably isn't worth the cost. Of course, there are personal reasons to get an education, such as to improve life satisfaction or to change industries. However, the financial reasons should also be considered, no matter your Wealth Level.

What about students graduating from high school? Do they need to be in Level 2 before they consider getting an advanced education? Of course not. Though nearly all high school students are in Level 1 with little wealth of their own, their families may not be. As a result, they can afford, by extension of their families, to take the risk of paying for an education. This doesn't mean that the cost of their education doesn't matter. But they do have a safety net if things don't go as planned. Unfortunately, this isn't the case for all high school students. Some take out student loans without any support to get a degree that doesn't increase their earnings. Then they end up trapped in Level 1 under a mountain of student debt. If you are a student whose family is in Level 1, you have to be extra careful about how much you pay for school.

This is why there is an educational sweet spot in Level 2. Because those in Level 2 have enough money to take some risks and move forward if it doesn't work out. This is especially true for those who pulled themselves out of Level 1 *without* an education. While these people can't go back in time to attend college, they do have other options at their disposal. If you find yourself in this situation, there is more you can do to increase your skills than you might imagine. For example, you could attend night classes, go to trade school, or pay for a skills-based boot camp. While you can learn many things on the job, some roles still call for specialized knowledge. This explains why the top twenty-five best-paying jobs in the U.S. in 2024 all required at least a bachelor's degree, according to *U.S. News & World Report*. In fact, among these top-paying roles, more than two thirds required a graduate degree and most were in the medical field.[2]

If we examine the median income among U.S. households

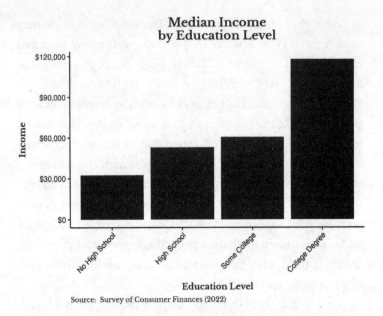

Median Income by Education Level

Source: Survey of Consumer Finances (2022)

by education level, you'll see the same thing. The typical U.S. household with more education has higher earnings than those with less education.[3]

The median household income for U.S. households with a high school education was around $53,000 in 2022, but it was nearly $118,000 for those with a college degree. This doesn't imply that a college degree *by itself* is responsible for this difference in earnings. However, this disparity in earnings by education level is found throughout the Wealth Ladder. For example, when we look at the median household income by education level *and* wealth level, for Levels 1–4, we see that more education is still correlated with higher earnings.

In Levels 1–4, the typical household with a college degree has a higher income than those with only a high school educa-

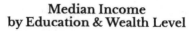

Median Income
by Education & Wealth Level

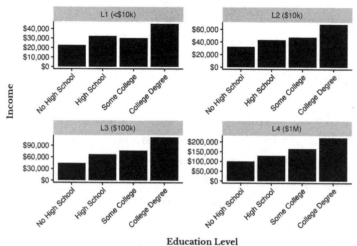

Education Level
Source: Survey of Consumer Finances (2022)

tion. This illustrates that there is some earnings premium associated with those who have a college degree, regardless of current wealth.

Additionally, although getting an education can cost you in the short run, it is likely to have a positive impact on your income in the long run. According to research published by the Brookings Institution, "the larger the student debt balance, the more the student tends to earn."[4] This is partially explained by professional schools (i.e., law, medicine, etc.) that charge exceptionally high tuition to access these higher-paying careers. I generally don't recommend taking out lots of debt for an education, but there are some cases where it can make sense.

Either way, if you want access to higher-paying jobs, you'll need to have the right education. Because education is a form of leverage. But instead of leveraging other people's time or other people's money, as we discussed in chapter 2, you leverage your own knowledge. In this way, your education can be thought of as an asset, like a stock or bond. But it's an even better asset than either of those, because no one can take it away from you. Your education is an asset that will pay you dividends for the rest of your life. Once you have it, you can do higher-value work and get paid more indefinitely. In other words, learn today, earn forever.

This is how you increase your income, save more money, and get out of Level 2 permanently. Getting an education is about working smarter, not harder. It's about generating a higher return on your most scarce resource—your time.

Unfortunately, this requires more effort than you'd think. Taking night classes while working a full-time job or attending a twelve-week coding boot camp can be challenging. This is particularly true if you have family to support. So where should you start? How do you make the right choice for your education and, ultimately, your career? How do you decide what to work on? While I don't have perfect answers to these questions, there's a great framework that you can use to get closer to them.

What you choose to do in your career is one of the most important decisions you will make in your life. It will determine what you think about, who you interact with, and how you build your wealth. But finding the right career is a modern problem. Throughout most of history, work meant hunting, gathering, or farming for the vast majority of people. Work was about survival, plain and simple. It's only in the last few hundred years that most of humanity has freed itself from this kind of existence. As of 2021, only 27 percent of the world's population still works in agriculture.[5]

As a result, most of us must decide what to do with our lives. Paul Graham, the founder of Y Combinator, wrote an essay titled "How to Do Great Work" that provides a useful starting point. As he says, "The work you choose needs to have three qualities: it has to be something you have a natural aptitude for, that you have a deep interest in, and that offers scope to do great work."[6] I'd reformulate Graham's third point to be "what people will pay for" instead. Not only is this more concrete, but it also reflects what work represents to most people—a way to earn money. As much as I want you to work on whatever you like, the reality is that you have to support yourself as well. With Graham's framework in mind, what you choose to work on should be at the intersection of:

- What you're good at
- What you're interested in
- What people will pay for

While you don't have to have all three of these qualities in the work you do, you should have at least two of them. Let's look at each pairing to see why.

What You're Good At + What You're Interested In

If you work on something that you're good at and that you're interested in, you will probably find a way to make money on it. Maybe not today, but eventually. This describes the journey of YouTuber James "Jimmy" Donaldson, aka MrBeast. Donaldson started his channel in 2012 when he was just fourteen years old by posting videos about Minecraft and other video games. This wasn't just a fun side project for Donaldson though. He wanted to make a career out of it. So he studied the YouTube algorithm for a thousand days to get better at making videos. In that time, he examined every detail about what it takes to make a great YouTube video. He analyzed a video's pacing, the brightness of its thumbnail, what made it go viral, and much more. As Donaldson once stated on a podcast, "I hardly had any friends because I was so obsessed with YouTube."[7]

Thankfully, Donaldson's obsession paid off. Today, MrBeast is one of the most popular channels on YouTube, with over 250 million subscribers as of May 2024. Donaldson has founded multiple consumer food businesses and a few global charities as a result of his YouTube fame. Across all his companies, he brings in $700 million a year in revenue.[8]

While you may never have $700 million a year in revenue, following your strengths and interests can pay off in smaller ways as well. This describes my journey blogging at OfDollarsAnd Data.com. I've always loved personal finance and was a decent writer, so back in 2017 I decided to start blogging. Each week I used data to write about a different topic in personal finance and investing. And while I didn't make any money on the blog for the first three years, I enjoyed the process. Eventually, though, I did start to make some money. It began with web ads, then I did a few brand partnerships, and it progressed from there. These are all things I never could've imagined when I first started writing online.

While working on something you're good at and interested in sounds appealing, you should consider the possible downsides as well. For example, chasing your strengths and interests can be stressful. Without another source of income, how will you survive? This is why I recommend keeping such an endeavor as a side project. Until it pays the bills, you will need to have some other money coming in the door to support your lifestyle. If that means working a job that you don't necessarily love to stay afloat, that's fine. Do something to keep the lights on for now. How long will you need to do this before your passion project starts making money? Unfortunately, there's no way to tell. It may never make money. But if you truly love it, how much does that matter?

There's a great irony in doing what you're good at and interested in—if you don't do it for the money you're *more likely* to make money. Think about it. If you do something because you love it and are good at it, you will stick with it through thick and thin. You will progress faster than your peers, and you will have a higher chance of becoming great. And in doing so, you will increase your chance of making money from it. So keep at it. Because if you can manage to make money off your strengths and interests, then you've hit the jackpot.

What You're Good At + What People Will Pay For

If you work on things that you're good at that people will pay for, there's a decent chance that you'll become interested in them as well. As Scott Galloway stated in *The Algebra of Wealth*:

> Your mission is to find something you're good at and apply the thousands of hours of grit and sacrifice to become great at it. As you get there, the feeling of growth and your

increasing mastery of your craft, along with the economic rewards, recognition, and camaraderie, will make you passionate about whatever "it" is.[9]

I wholeheartedly support this notion as a writer who used to hate the act of writing. Thankfully, as readers told me how much they enjoyed my work, I came to love writing in a way I never thought possible. If you're deciding whether to focus on what you're good at or what you're interested in, go for what you're good at first. You may just find that your interests change as a result.

What You're Interested In + What People Will Pay For

Lastly, if you work on things that you are interested in that people will pay for, you may eventually get good at them. This explains why many people who are great at something tend to have a deep interest in the field. Otherwise, they would've given up as soon as they hit obstacles on their journey. But obstacles are merely a filter that keep the uninterested from becoming great. While following your interests isn't guaranteed to lead to such success, being a part of something you care about has its own satisfactions. After all, if it pays the bills and you love it, how much do you really care about being great at it?

———

No matter what you choose to work on, finding the intersection of your strengths, interests, and what people pay for is essential for developing a successful career. Of course, the difficult part is figuring out where to start. Should you focus on your strengths, your interests, or what people will pay for first? If I had to pick, I'd say you should pursue a career that people will pay you for. Of the three, it's the only one that is required to get by. After all, you don't have to be good at something or interested in it to do it. But you do need to make money. Once you have some income, then you can focus on finding the career that best suits your strengths and interests.

Following this strategy is also the most effective way to get out of Level 2. Because in Level 2 you don't have to stress about where your next meal is coming from. You don't have to worry as much about an unlucky break sending you into a downward spiral. But you should consider the work you do and how that work will help you build wealth in the long run. Failing to do so is what keeps people in Level 2.

If you look at the income in each Wealth Level from the 2022 Survey of Consumer Finances, this becomes quite apparent. For example, the median (i.e., typical) income for U.S. households in Level 2 is $47,560, compared to $83,230 in Level 3. Households in the *bottom* 25 percent of earners in Level 3 earn roughly the same as the median household in Level 2. If we go further up the Wealth Ladder, this becomes even more skewed. For example, U.S. households in the bottom 10 percent of earners in Level 4 earn about $20,000 per year *more than* the median household in Level 2. As we saw in chapter 2, there are few households with high wealth and low income.

The opposite is also true—there aren't many households with low wealth and high income. Only slightly more than a quarter of U.S. households in Level 2 earn more than $70,000 per year. For the record, $70,000 is the median income across *all* households within the United States. Additionally, a little over 10 percent of households in Level 2 earn more than six figures.[10] Why are there so few households in Level 2 with high incomes? Because once you have a high-enough income, it's much easier to get out of Level 2. Therefore, the only households in Level 2 with high incomes will be outliers in one way or another. Either they just started earning more and haven't had time to build wealth, or they spend too much of their income and fail to build wealth. Regardless, these households are the exception, not the rule. As the data suggests, households with higher incomes tend to be further up the Wealth Ladder.

This is why failing to focus on your career (and thus, your income) is the financial sin of Level 2. Without such focus, it will take you much longer to climb the Wealth Ladder. The problem some people run into in Level 2 is fixating too much on what they're doing instead of what they're *not* doing. Many people only think they've made a mistake when they see a negative outcome in their life. But this is just one kind of mistake you can make. You can also make a mistake by missing out on a more positive outcome. As discussed in chapter 2, the opportunity costs of your career decisions can be easily overlooked. But they exist nonetheless.

After all, you can be in Level 2 with a dead-end job and feel fine. You get a small raise every few years. You pay all your bills. Nothing is wrong. But if you want more out of your financial life, then the mistake you are making is in the career you aren't pursuing. It's in the life you aren't living. It's easy to miss this because the consequences of your actions aren't visible and readily apparent to you. Rather, they only show up as opportunity costs, or paths not taken.

How do you know if you are making such a mistake by being in a dead-end job? Consider the following: Are you learning new skills? Is there a clear path for advancement? Have you been given any new responsibilities lately? Has your pay gone up in recent years?

If the answer to these questions is mostly no, then you should start pursuing the career that you want as soon as possible. Because these sorts of decisions can have huge long-term effects. As Sam Altman, the CEO of OpenAI and creator of ChatGPT, stated on the *Y Combinator* podcast:

> Compound interest is a good metaphor here. If you work really hard at the beginning of your career, and you get a little bit better at what you do every day, every month, every week, and you learn more, and you meet more people, and you just get more done, there is a compound effect. And it's far better to put that time in at the beginning of your career than at the end. Because if you do it at the beginning, you get to benefit from it for the rest of the time you work. . . . So obviously you don't want to work all the time because your twenties are your twenties, but I do think you want to work harder than most people think you should. . . . Working hard early in your career to get the leverage and the compounding effects is underrated and one of the most valuable pieces of advice that I never got.[11]

Changing your career trajectory, as Altman recommends, is the best way out of Level 2. Not only does it make logical sense about how such a decision can pay off, but the income and wealth data support it. Unfortunately, this can be a challenge. The primary problem with changing your career trajectory is figuring out what to change it to. While there are no perfect answers, focusing on a combination of your strengths, interests, and what people will pay for is the right way to go.

Level 2 Summary

- **Follow-Up:** Identify the intersection of your strengths, interests, and what people will pay you for.

- **Opportunities:** Get an education that offers the possibility of higher-paying work.

- **Risks:** Dead-end jobs. Ignoring your opportunity costs.

- **Mental framework:** Learn today, earn forever.

As much as compounding can help throughout your career in Level 2, it can be even more powerful when it comes to your investments. This is what we turn our attention to in Level 3.

CHAPTER 6

Level 3 ($100k–$1M)

———

Just Keep Buying

E very 175 years something remarkable happens—Jupiter, Saturn, Uranus, and Neptune come into close alignment. An American aerospace engineer by the name of Gary Flandro discovered this while working at NASA's Jet Propulsion Laboratory in the summer of 1964. More importantly, Flandro realized that the next time this alignment would occur would be in the late 1970s, a little more than a decade away.[1]

As a result of his finding, Flandro devised a grand planetary tour that would allow a probe to fly by all four gas giants much faster and more cheaply than previously estimated. The physics behind the tour required using the planets as slingshots, also known as gravity assists, in order to cut down on energy costs and the time needed to visit them. The end result was NASA's Voyager program. After considering ten thousand possible trajectories, NASA decided upon two of them and launched Voyager 2 followed by Voyager 1 in the late summer of 1977.

Two things stand out about the Voyager program. First, decisions made by NASA scientists forty years ago have had a profound effect on the mission and its success right to the present day. For example, despite launching after Voyager 2, Voyager 1 is currently the furthest man-made object from the Earth. As of mid-2024, Voyager 1 was over 15 billion miles (or 22 light hours) from our home planet. And that distance is increasing— every second, Voyager 1 moves ten miles farther away from us. Tick. Tick. Ti—Voyager 1 just completed a marathon. The decision to have Voyager 1 start on a faster and shorter trajectory and then let nature run its course made this possible. All it took was some great decision making; the rest was physics.

The second thing that stands out about the Voyager program is how once a successful process is put in place, the end results can be surprising. What started as a mission to check out the gas giants and their respective moons became a study of the edge of our solar system and deep space. Voyager 1 has sent back useful data to NASA since its launch in 1977. The goals achieved by the Voyager missions were ones that were not necessarily imagined at the outset.

These two ideas from the Voyager program are highly relevant to your finances in Level 3 of the Wealth Ladder, because Level 3 is where the way you approach your investments can transform your future wealth. The reasoning for this is simple math. Someone with $100,000 invested will earn ten times more than someone with $10,000 invested, all else being equal. But even when all else isn't equal, the person with more money invested can still win out. This is because a 2 percent return on $100,000 is bigger than a 10 percent return on $10,000. The higher investment amount more than makes up for the lower overall return. As you invest larger sums of money up the Wealth Ladder, this becomes even more true.

Of course, I am not saying that you need to wait until Level 3 before you can start investing. I recommend that everyone invest as soon as they comfortably can. However, those in Level 3 (and above) will miss out on more by not investing. This is especially true the longer they wait to get invested. We can illustrate this with a simple example.

Imagine someone who saves $10,000 a year for forty years while earning 7 percent on their money. At the end of the forty years, they will have roughly $2 million in their portfolio, though they only contributed $400,000 ($10,000 * 40) in total. This means that $400,000 of their final portfolio value was related to the contributions they made, while the remaining $1.6 million came from the growth of those investments.

However, not every investment they made grew to the same amount. In fact, their first $10,000 contribution eventually grew to $140,000, or 7 percent of the final $2 million portfolio value. This is true despite only being 2.5 percent (1/40) of the contributions. Why did this happen? Because it had more time to grow and compound on itself. You can see this clearly in the image on the following page showing the total percentage that each annual contribution made to the final portfolio value.

In this case, earlier investments end up contributing more to the final portfolio than later investments. This is why the investment in year 1 ends up being 7 percent of the final total while the investment in year 30 ends up being less than 1% of the final total.

Nevertheless, a bigger point is lurking just beneath the surface. If we add these bars up over time and show the *cumulative* total of the final portfolio by year, we find something remark-

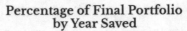

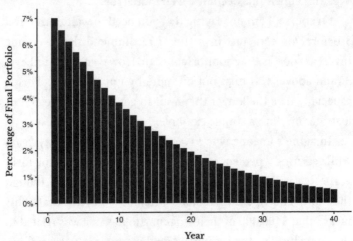

Source: Simulated data (OfDollarsAndData.com)
Note: Assumes constant savings for 40 years and a 7% annual rate of return.

able. Not only does the first year contribute 7 percent to the final total, but the first ten years of contributions make up over half of the final portfolio value! You can see this more clearly in the chart on the next page showing the cumulative percentage of the final portfolio based on number of years invested.

In this instance, the first ten years of contributions make a bigger overall impact on the final portfolio value than the final thirty years of contributions. This demonstrates how counterintuitive compounding can be, because compounding isn't a linear process. With a linear process, every action you take has an *equal* impact on the outcome. For example, running a marathon is a linear process. Assuming you have a constant stride length, your first step in the marathon contributes just as much as your last step.

Over Half the Final Portfolio Is Built in the First Decade of Saving

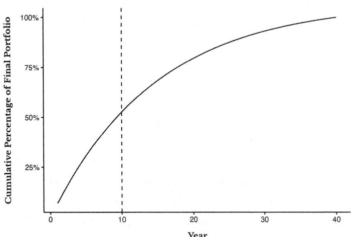

Source: Simulated data (OfDollarsAndData.com)
Note: Assumes constant savings for 40 years and a 7% annual rate of return.

But compounding isn't like this. Compounding is an exponential process in which actions taken earlier in time have a bigger impact than those taken later in time. For example, imagine a marathon where your stride length increased by 10 percent with every step you took. Your first step might be 2.3 feet (0.7 meters). Then your second step would be 2.53 feet (0.77 meters), or 10 percent longer. Your third step would be 2.783 feet (0.847 meters), or 10 percent longer than the second step, and so forth. If this is how running worked, you would finish a marathon in less than 100 steps, compared to the 50,000 steps it typically takes. But here's the part that's counterintuitive— your final step to finish the marathon would be roughly 2.5 miles (around 4 kilometers) in length. And every step you took before it helped contribute to its vast length. We both know that this is physically impossible, but in the context of our example, this is how an exponential process works. Actions build upon themselves. This is why investing earlier in time can give you such an edge. By doing so, you essentially lock in more time for your money to earn money. And if you start early enough, you can be far less disciplined later.

I've previously called this idea "Go Big, Then Stop" because it highlights how you can invest more earlier in time, stop contributing later, and still do fine.[2] Unfortunately, if you want to get to Level 4 of the Wealth Ladder, you'll probably have to "Go Big" and keep going. In our previous example, our hypothetical investor finished with a $2 million portfolio after forty years of investing. How long did it take for them to get to $1 million? Over thirty years! This illustrates the power of investing *and* consistency when it comes to building wealth. This was the key insight from my first book, *Just Keep Buying: Proven Ways to Save Money and Build Your Wealth*. That book was meant for those in Levels 2–3 who wanted to get to Levels 3–4 of the Wealth Ladder. This makes Just Keep Buying a Level 2–3 strategy. Though you could use Just Keep Buying to ascend beyond Level 4, such an outcome is unlikely without a *very* high income, an extended time horizon, or both. As a result, you will probably need to use a higher-level strategy. We will explore this more in the next chapter. For now, if you want to get out of Level 3, start investing.

Once you've started on your investment journey, you still have to figure out what to invest in. Unfortunately, there is no right answer. I've read more than one hundred books on investing since 2012 and have been writing on the topic for nearly a decade, but still haven't found a one-size-fits-all solution. While this might sound unsatisfying, it's the truth. I know people who have gotten wealthy through real estate, stocks, their own businesses, and much more. What matters is finding the investments that are right for you. For example, some like owning and managing physical assets such as real estate. Others prefer the low maintenance of stock index funds and ETFs. Some like running their own businesses. Others choose to invest in private businesses and let others manage them. And so forth. But despite their many differences, all these investors have one thing in common—they own income-producing assets. These include:

- Stocks/equities
- Bonds/fixed income
- Real estate/rental properties
- Farmland
- Small businesses
- Royalties
- Their own businesses/products

There are pros and cons to investing in each of these that I've discussed in my prior work. For now, focus on learning more about these asset classes before deciding where to invest. Once again, there is no right answer here, just a series of trade-offs. The fact that you are considering buying income-producing assets is what matters. As I mentioned in chapter 3, income-producing assets are the key differentiator between those higher and those lower on the Wealth Ladder. While this isn't the only distinction between these groups, it's the one that stands out the most on their personal balance sheets.

But investing isn't the only way to get to Level 4 on the Wealth

Ladder. You can also get there by starting a successful side hustle. A side hustle is a business venture that you do *in addition* to your primary job to earn extra money. Side hustles can be as simple as pet sitting or doing freelance work (e.g., consulting, design, etc.). They could also be as complex as creating physical products or launching an online business. The possibilities are truly endless, and there is no limit to how much you could earn from a side hustle. To prove my point, let me tell you about two of the most unique side hustles I've ever heard of.

The first involves the William Preston Lane Jr. Memorial Bridge, or what is informally known as the Chesapeake Bay Bridge, in Maryland. When the bridge was completed in 1952, it was the "largest continuous over-water steel structure" in the world, measuring over four miles in length.[3] Due to its immense height and narrow roadway, *Travel + Leisure* magazine ranked it one of the scariest bridges in the world. The ranking was not unwarranted. After a series of accidents on the bridge, many residents became too afraid to cross it. Enter Alex Robinson. Robinson founded the Kent Island Express, a business that drives nervous locals over the Chesapeake Bay Bridge for a fee. One man used Robinson's service for eight years to get to and from work. By 2013, the Kent Island Express had nearly six thousand customers paying $25 per crossing.[4] What started as a side project for Robinson became a full-fledged business doing six figures in annual revenue.

While the Kent Island Express is noteworthy, the most unique side hustle I ever saw was at the Mall of America in 2024. It was a Saturday morning and my friend Darren and I noticed a crowd forming around a large stage at the base of the mall's four-story rotunda. In front of the stage was a pool of water, and inside the pool was a squirrel waterskiing behind a miniature remote-controlled boat. The screen above the stage read "Twiggy: The Waterskiing Squirrel." I couldn't believe my eyes. There I was in the largest mall in America alongside thousands of others watching a waterskiing squirrel . . . for free. I later found out that Twiggy's Inc., the business behind Twiggy, had been around since 1979 and was still family owned and operated. They started after Chuck and Lou Ann Best rescued a baby squirrel during a hurricane in Florida. They kept the squirrel as a pet and took it with them whenever they went boating. This is how Chuck got the idea to train it to water ski. After a local paper heard about Twiggy, the rest was history. Twiggy and her successors have done shows throughout the U.S., Canada, and Europe for decades. In addition to their live performances, Twiggy's Inc. also sells merchandise with taglines like "Getting Twiggy With It" and "That Squirrel Can Water Ski!" While I don't know the financials behind Twiggy's Inc., the business has been able to support a family for two generations and has grown in recent years.[5]

The Kent Island Express and Twiggy's Inc. both demonstrate the many possibilities that exist when it comes to making money via a side hustle. And while you may not have a scary bridge in your town or a woodland creature that you can train to do watersports, there are many other moneymaking opportunities out there. For example, here are some of the things I've seen people do for extra cash:

- Part-time tutoring
- Freelance photography

- Flipping items online
- Chasing credit card rewards

And the list goes on. I have a relative who 3D prints portable diesel heaters and sells them on Etsy. He makes good side money doing it too.

The best thing about a side hustle is that it can typically be done on nights and weekends, when it won't interfere with your day job. And if you have no plans to replace your day job, the extra cash generated by your side hustle can help you build wealth more quickly.

Whether you are investing or doing a side hustle, the key is to generate more income streams. Most people have just one income stream—their job. If they lose that single source of income, they're in trouble. By investing and pursuing a side hustle, you diversify your income streams and reduce risk in your financial life. While it may not fully replace your need for a job, it can make a big difference over time.

Regardless of which investments or side hustles you choose to pursue (if any), the way out of Level 3 is more income. We can see this clearly in the Panel Study of Income Dynamics (PSID), conducted by the University of Michigan, which followed the same set of U.S. households from 1968 to 2021.[6] As a result, we know how these households climbed the Wealth Ladder. For example, if we were to separate households that went from Level 3 to Level 4 versus those that stayed in Level 3 from 1984 to 1994, their biggest difference was their *starting* income. The average starting income of households that stayed in Level 3 after a decade was $98,905 (in 2021 dollars). However, the average starting income for households that started in Level 3 but made it to Level 4 was $150,185. That's a 52 percent higher income at the start of the period!

More importantly, the households that made it to Level 4 also saw more inflation-adjusted *income growth* over the subsequent decade. The households that stayed in Level 3 saw their average inflation-adjusted income grow by 27 percent (to $125,832) over ten years. However, those that made it to Level 4 increased their average inflation-adjusted income by 43 percent (to $214,865) over the same period.[7] This illustrates how those who make it to Level 4 tend to have higher starting incomes and higher income growth than those who stay in Level 3.

If increasing your income is the way up the Wealth Ladder in Level 3, then not controlling your spending is the way down. Going back to the PSID data, we can examine a household's overall spending from 1999 through 2021. And once we know a household's spending, we can see whether it had any impact on their wealth level over time. Unsurprisingly, households that spent a higher percentage of their income were more likely to end up *down* a wealth level after ten years. From 1999 to 2021, the average starting income of households that stayed in Level 3 after a decade was $113,876 (in 2021 dollars), and their average annual after-tax spending at the start of the decade was around $55,233. However, households in Level 3 that fell to Level 2 after a decade had an average starting income of $88,631, but average starting spending of $52,532. This means that the households that fell from Level 3 to Level 2 over a decade spent 59 percent of their pretax income annually compared to only 49 percent for those that stayed in Level 3. In other words, households that fell to Level 2 made about $25,000 *less than* those who stayed in Level 3, but they spent nearly the same!

We see the same thing for those households that started in Level 2 and fell to Level 1 compared to those that started and stayed in Level 2 after a decade. Those that stayed in Level 2 earned $65,336 and spent $37,847. But those that fell to Level 1 earned $61,662 and spent $38,970. Level 2 households that fell to Level 1 made less *and* spent more than those who stayed in Level 2 after a decade.[8]

In general, spending tends to increase as income increases. This is true across the Wealth Ladder. However, spending tends to increase *at a slower rate* than income. This means that spending as a percentage of income should decline as you move up the Wealth Ladder. And it does! The only exception is for households that end up falling down the Wealth Ladder. Fortunately, falling down the Wealth Ladder is quite rare. For example, only 10 percent of households that started in Level 3 were in Levels 1–2 after ten years. And for those households that started in Level 2, about 17 percent ended up in Level 1 over the same period. This is empirical proof that overspending can wreak havoc on your financial life, if you let it.

Where does this overspending tend to occur? Though it can vary, for those in Level 3, the primary culprit tends to be housing. As we saw in chapter 3, homeowners in Level 3 tend to have nearly 65 percent of their assets, on average, in their home. Although you can look at your home as an investment, in many ways it is a consumption good. It's something that generally costs you money, not something that makes you money.

More importantly, Level 3 is where homeownership is almost universal, at least in the United States. While only 6 percent of households in Level 1 and 42 percent of households in Level 2 own their own home, 90 percent of households in Level

3 do. So not only are you very likely to buy a home in Level 3, but you are likely going to spend a good portion of your assets doing it as well.

Being mindful of how much you spend on your primary residence will have a huge financial impact down the road. As I will explore in more depth later, 61.8 percent of people in Level 3 will still be in Level 3 after twenty years. While going from $100,000 to $1 million isn't easy, overspending on big-ticket items like your car or home surely won't help.

Though overspending only impacts a smaller percentage of households, make sure that you aren't one of them. If you do that and focus on increasing your income (through investments, side hustles, or both), then Level 4 will be here sooner than you think.

Level 3 Summary

- **Follow-Up:** Research which investments are right for you. Consider side hustles to earn more income.

- **Opportunities:** Invest in income-producing assets and develop more income streams.

- **Risks:** Overspending on big-ticket items.

- **Mental framework:** Just Keep Buying.

Now that we've looked at some of the ways to progress in Level 3, let's explore why Level 4 may be the hardest wealth level to escape.

CHAPTER 7

Level 4 ($1M–$10M)

What Got You Here Won't Get You There

n 1982, the richest country in the world on a per-person basis was one you have probably never heard of. Situated in the Central Pacific, northeast of Australia, the island nation of Nauru was rolling in the dough. The reason for their riches? Phosphate, and lots of it. At the time, Nauru was the largest exporter of phosphate in the world, to the tune of $400 million per year (in 2024 dollars). On a per-person basis this equated to $88,000 for every Nauru resident.[1] To ensure that the country remained wealthy even after its phosphate reserves ran out, the Nauru Phosphate Royalties Trust (NPRT) was set up to manage and invest its income. Initially, this plan worked. By 1991, the NPRT had over $3 billion in assets (in 2024 dollars).[2]

However, as phosphate exports began to decline in the 1990s, Nauru officials became desperate to generate additional income. In 1993, the NPRT invested millions of dollars into *Leonardo the Musical*. This was a London-based theatrical production that went on to become a massive flop. There were also investments in various real estate projects that didn't turn out as planned. Nauru even began selling banking licenses, turning the island nation into a hub for tax evasion and money laundering. Despite these attempts to slow the depletion of the NPRT, by 2004 its assets had declined to $50 million (in 2024 dollars).[3]

There are many parallels between the island nation of Nauru and those in Level 4 of the Wealth Ladder. Just like Nauru used its excessive income to save money, households in Level 4 tend to have high incomes that allow them to save as well. However, where Nauru made a mistake was in how it *invested* those savings after it earned them. The same thing can happen to households in Level 4 of the Wealth Ladder if they aren't careful. Because in Level 4, your investment decisions are amplified by your wealth. This is true both on the upside *and* the downside. While losing 10 percent in Level 3 equates to a loss of $10,000 at a minimum, in Level 4 that loss would become $100,000. When converted into absolute dollars, something that is unfortunate in Level 3 is catastrophic in Level 4. Why does this transition occur? Because Level 4 is the first wealth level in which most of your wealth is likely to be in income-producing assets. As we saw in chapter 3, on average, 53 percent of the total assets of households in Level 4 were income-producing assets. These are the kinds of assets that can fluctuate wildly in value. It also explains why investment mistakes matter more in Level 4 and above.

While few investors have the courage to talk about such mistakes publicly, they do happen. Noah Kagan, an entrepreneur, tweeted about how he lost $100,000 in a real estate deal, though the original proposal aimed for a yearly cash return of 11 percent.[4] I don't mean to pick on real estate investors, because such losses can happen in other asset classes as well. For example, an analysis from Morningstar found that Cathie Wood's Ark funds destroyed over $14 billion in shareholder value from 2014 to 2023.[5] These funds focused primarily on highly speculative technology stocks that did incredibly well from 2020 to 2021. Unfortunately, these same stocks took massive losses in 2022. Though Cathie Wood's Ark funds couldn't be more different from an individual real estate deal, they both have one thing in common—concentration. Kagan's real estate was concentrated in a particular location while Wood's Ark funds were concentrated in a particular industry. And when you have too much concentration, all it takes is one unlucky break for things to unravel.

We will talk more about the risk of concentrated positions in the next chapter, but for now, the solution is simple—diversify your portfolio. Unfortunately, many investors may think they are diversified when they are not. Just because you own many different rental properties or many different stocks, that doesn't mean you are diversified. For example, if you own ten stocks in the oil and gas industry and one of them is charged with accounting fraud, you're diversified. However, if you own ten stocks in the oil and gas industry and the price of oil falls off a cliff, you aren't diversified. See the difference? If you have rental properties all in the same city or stocks all in the same sector, you have a concentration problem. This is why, if you want to remain in Level 4, you must diversify your investments.

Focusing on your investments is the mental shift you need to make in Level 4, because Level 4 is the point where your investment portfolio is likely to earn you more than you could by working. For example, imagine having a job that pays you

$250,000 a year. This would put you in the top 10 percent of U.S. households in 2022. After tax, let's assume you take home $170,000 per year. If you save half of this, it means that your job adds $85,000 to your wealth each year. Now also imagine having $2 million invested across all your financial accounts. A 5 percent return on your money would generate $100,000 in wealth. This exceeds what you can save in a year by working!

As your portfolio continues to grow, the earnings from your job will have a hard time keeping up. This doesn't mean that you should stop saving money once your investments reach a certain size. However, you should shift your focus to where it will have the biggest impact. In Level 4, that usually means changing how you manage your investments. After all, if you made it to Level 4, you probably don't have a spending problem. It would be hard to get there if you did. But once you're in Level 4, your investments will likely have the biggest impact on your annual change in wealth.

Unfortunately, while sensible investments will help you grow your wealth in Level 4, they are unlikely to get you to Level 5 ($10M–$100M) and beyond. The data supports this conclusion. As we will explore in more detail later, 64 percent of households in Level 4 will still be in Level 4 two decades from now. Only 8 percent of households that start in Level 4 make it to Level 5 after twenty years. Level 4 is the hardest level to break out of for good reason—the strategy needed to get out is drastically different from the strategy needed to get in.

To get to Level 4, the strategy is straightforward but not easy. You need sufficiently high income in excess of your spending, some good investments, or a combination of the two. However, to get to Level 5 requires a different skill set altogether. It is unlikely that you will get there through a job alone, even if you are very successful and work at it for a long time. We can show this with some simple math.

Imagine you just hit Level 4 and you have $1 million in investments. If you don't save another dollar and your investments return 5 percent per year (after inflation), it would take forty-seven years for you to get to $10 million. Of course, you probably aren't going to stop saving once you hit $1 million. So let's assume you save $100,000 after tax per year, a significant sum of money. How long would it take you to get to $10 million with a 5 percent annual return? Twenty-eight years. What about if you saved $200,000 per year? Then it would take about twenty-one years. What about if you saved $300,000 annually? It still takes seventeen years!

As you can see, even with a very high-paying job (e.g., $500,000 per year or more), it will take multiple decades to get to Level 5. And note that this would be *after* you've already made it to Level 4. If you manage to get to Level 4 in your thirties or forties, this is doable, but will still require a lot of effort. Unfortunately, as I will cover later, only 5 percent of people in their thirties and 15 percent of people in their forties are in Level 4. Since the median age for those in Level 4 is sixty-two, most people don't enter Level 4 until later in life. This means that the typical person in Level 4 would need to work an extremely demanding job into their seventies and eighties to get to Level 5. And who wants to do that?

This is why it's so easy to feel stuck in Level 4. You can have a lucrative career and millions of dollars in net worth, but any financial progress you make is almost unnoticeable. As I discussed in chapter 1, Level 4 is the wealth level where you begin to have "Travel freedom." You can stay in nicer hotels or upgrade to first class more often, but it's not like you can afford to charter a superyacht. Life in Level 4 isn't Ferraris, mansions, and daily caviar. And an extra $1 million in wealth won't change that. For example, going from $4 million to $5 million in wealth doesn't allow you to transform your spending in any significant way. You can't suddenly fly private all the time or upgrade to a much fancier house. Yes, you can take more vacations or pay for your children's education, but your life (as a whole) won't feel all that different. I know this sounds out of touch, but it's true. It reminds me of that scene from *Succession* where Cousin Greg is convinced that he is "golden" after learning of his $5 million inheritance. That's when Connor Roy tells him the unfortunate truth:

> You can't do anything with five [million], Greg. Five's a nightmare . . . Can't retire. Not worth it to work. Oh, yes. Five will drive you un poco loco, my fine-feathered friend. The poorest rich person in America.[6]

While *Succession* was being a bit humorous here, there is a bit of truth to their joke. Because Level 4 is where many traditional career paths start losing their effectiveness. They don't move the needle for your wealth as much anymore. For example, when you have $1 million in wealth, saving $100,000 increases your wealth by 10 percent. But by the time you have $5 million, that same $100,000 in savings only increases your wealth by 2 percent. And that percentage will continue to decline as you move further up Level 4. To increase your wealth by 10 percent when you have $5 million, you would need to save $500,000.

Once you consider taxes and cost of living, you'd have to make more than $1 million annually to pull this off. This income level would put you near the top 1 percent of all households in the United States. Not impossible, but clearly not easy either.

Thankfully, there is a better way. As I just illustrated, a high-paying job, decent investments, and a good savings rate can get you into Level 4. However, it probably won't get you out of Level 4. As Marshall Goldsmith, an American executive leadership coach, was known to say, "What got you here won't get you there."[7] Unless you are a celebrity (i.e., actor, musician, professional athlete, etc.), your job likely won't generate enough income to get you to Level 5. But do you know what could? Starting or joining a business that eventually sells for a lot of money. In either case, you will need to focus on getting one thing—equity. You either need a little equity in a very large business or a lot of equity in a smaller business. And that business needs to sell for millions of dollars (or more) or generate lots of annual income. Either way, getting that equity will be one of the most important financial decisions of your life. As Felix Dennis stated in *How to Get Rich*:

> To become rich, every single percentage point of anything you own is crucial. It is worth fighting for, tooth and claw. It is worth suing for. It is worth shouting and banging the table for. It is worth begging for and groveling for. It is worth lying and cheating for. In extremis, it is even worth negotiating for. Never, never, never, never hand over a single share of anything you have acquired or created if you can help it.[8]

While lying and cheating for equity is not a strategy I would recommend, owning a business is your ticket to Level 5. This explains why households in Level 5 have, on average, 31 percent of their assets in business interests.[9] And those businesses tend to generate lots of income. When the Harrison Group analyzed households with $500,000 or more in *discretionary* income—or income in excess of your basic necessities—they found that 63 percent of these households got their wealth from their own business or someone else's business they joined early on. The remaining households got their wealth from financial investments (17 percent), real estate (13 percent), inheritance (4 percent), or something else (3 percent).[10] As you can see, private business ownership is what drives wealth and income at the upper end of the spectrum. It's also the biggest differentiator between those in Level 4 and those in Levels 5–6 on the Wealth Ladder.

Of course, starting a successful business that you later sell for millions of dollars is easier said than done. It's also beyond the scope of this book. I've never created and sold a seven-figure business. However, I do know that any business you start will require leverage. As we saw in chapter 2, the four kinds of leverage are: labor, capital, content, and code. You'll have to harness some combination of these if you want a chance of getting to Level 5.

Why do you need leverage? Because you can't do everything yourself. As Alfred North Whitehead once wrote, "Civilization advances by extending the number of important operations which we can perform without thinking of them."[11] When you create a business with leverage, that is what you're doing. You are extending the number of things you can do without actually having to do them. You are separating your time from the creation of value.

When Mark Zuckerberg says that Meta/Facebook needs to build a new product, hundreds of people start working to make it happen. Zuckerberg doesn't have to manually write the code, test the code, launch the code, and maintain it over time. No, the business he created does it for him. Of course, this isn't free. He has to pay those people lots of money to do all that work. But if the product launch is successful, it can generate more value than what he paid them to create it. This is possible because Zuckerberg has so much leverage. If his employees create a successful product, it can be scaled to the billions of people on Meta's platforms all around the world. You and I can't do that because we don't have the same amount of leverage that he does.

Thankfully, you don't need that much leverage to get to Level 5. You just need to create something successful enough to break out of Level 4. You won't hear about many of these smaller businesses in the news, but they build wealth just the same. The hard part is figuring out what kind of business to start. Unfortunately, I can't give you the answer. You'll need to make that determination based on your skills, experience, and temperament.

Nevertheless, if you decide to start a business, there are a few things you'll need to consider. First, it's not for the faint of heart. As Elon Musk has been known to say, "Starting a business is like chewing glass and staring into the abyss." When people ask him what he can do to encourage entrepreneurs to start companies, he replies, "If you need encouragement, don't start a company."[12] You might think this is just a joke, but it's not. I've heard far too many ultrasuccessful people say something similar about running businesses. Jensen Huang, the CEO of Nvidia, was asked what company he would start if he was thirty years old again, and this was his response:

> I wouldn't do it. . . . The reason why I wouldn't do it, and it goes back to why it's so hard, is building a company and building Nvidia turned out to have been a million times harder than I expected it to be. . . . And, at the time, if we had realized the pain and suffering and just how vulnerable you are going to feel and the challenges that you are going to endure . . . I don't think anybody would start a company. Nobody in their right mind would do it.[13]

And this came from a guy whose net worth was over $40 billion at the time. It makes you think: If the successful entrepreneurs are telling you not to start a company, what would the unsuccessful ones say?

The second issue with starting a business is that it usually requires a significant amount of experience. Researchers at Northwestern University and MIT analyzed data from the U.S. Census Bureau and found the following:

> Successful entrepreneurs are much more likely to be middle-aged, not young. For the top 0.1 percent of fastest growing new businesses in the U.S., the average age of the founder in the business's first year was 45. Similarly, middle-aged founders dominate successful exits. By our estimation, a 50-year-old founder is 1.8 times more likely than a 30-year-old founder to create one of the

highest growth firms. Founders in their early 20s have the lowest likelihood of building a top-growth firm.[14]

The authors theorized that older founders were more successful because they had more financial resources, greater domain knowledge, and a larger network than younger founders. They also reported that working in a specific industry before starting a company "more than doubled" the chance of a successful exit.[15] So if you want to maximize the probability that your business does well, make sure you have industry experience and don't start it until you're in your forties. Though this still won't guarantee success, the evidence suggests that it's the best chance you've got to sell a successful business and make it to Level 5.

Another thing to think about before starting a business is whether you'll have a financial safety net to fall back on in case you fail. In other words, do you or your family have sufficient financial resources for you to take this risk? While I want to say wealth doesn't matter when it comes to starting a business, unfortunately, it does. Having a backup plan if things don't work out allows you to take bigger risks than someone who doesn't have the same resources. It reminds me of this anonymous Hacker News comment from November 2017:

> Entrepreneurship is like one of those carnival games where you throw darts or something. Middle-class kids can afford one throw. Most miss. A few hit the target and get a small prize. A very few hit the center bull's-eye and get a bigger prize. Rags to riches! The American

Dream lives on. Rich kids can afford many throws. If they want to, they can try over and over and over again until they hit something and feel good about themselves. Some keep going until they hit the center bull's-eye, then they give speeches or write blog posts about "meritocracy" and the salutary effects of hard work. Poor kids aren't visiting the carnival. They're the ones working it.[16]

While this comment might seem exaggerated to some, there is data to back it. A study from Israel's Finance Ministry found that "the income of someone's parents is the factor that correlates most to entrepreneurship, with higher wealth connected to a greater likelihood of being a start-up founder."[17] Many prominent tech billionaires, including Bill Gates and Jeff Bezos, had parental support in the creation of their first businesses.[18] Of course, I'm not suggesting that rich parents are a requirement to become a successful entrepreneur. However, having some sort of financial resources (whether your family's or your own) will make it much easier for you to start a company.

The last thing to consider before starting a business is whether your business will be an actual business or just a job in disguise. As Michael E. Gerber wrote in *The E-Myth Revisited*, "If your business depends on you, you don't own a business—you have a job."[19] When first starting out, obviously your business will depend on you. However, if you don't have a way to eventually remove yourself from the business, then you may be signing yourself up for a glorified job. While being your own boss has its perks, if you can't sell your business because it relies too much on you, then you have a problem. There's a difference between building a scalable business with leverage and trapping yourself in self-employment.

The goal of starting any business should be to create a valuable asset that you can eventually sell to someone else. So if that asset requires forty hours of weekly work on your behalf, then it will be far less attractive to investors. No one wants to buy a job from you, even if it is making a good profit every year. They want to buy a self-sustaining business that is mostly run by its employees. This is where using labor as leverage can really pay off and get you into Level 5. Obviously, it isn't easy to do, but it should be the eventual goal when you start your own company.

If I still haven't convinced you *not* to start a business, then it might be the right move for you. The nice thing about starting a business is that you don't have to go full time on it immediately. I've seen people start their business on the side and keep it that way until they reached a certain earnings threshold. For example, you could run your business part time until it completely replaces the income from your day job. Once you've reached that point, you'll have more proof of concept for your business and whether you can leave traditional employment behind. This isn't possible with all kinds of businesses, but having some validation before taking such a big leap can be helpful.

Level 4 has many perks, but it can also feel like financial limbo for those aiming to climb higher up the Wealth Ladder. As traditional employment proves less effective in building your wealth, it's easy to feel stuck or unmotivated. If you find yourself in this situation, you have two options: either accept that Level 5 may not be in your future and enjoy life, or reignite your passion, use more leverage, and create the life that you truly desire. The choice is yours.

> ## Level 4 Summary
>
> - **Follow-Up:** Accept remaining in Level 4 or consider starting or joining a business with equity upside potential.
>
> - **Opportunities:** Business ownership and continued investment.
>
> - **Risks:** Speculative investments. Starting a business that becomes a job.
>
> - **Mental framework:** What got you here won't get you there.

———

Now that we've looked at why Level 4 is the hardest wealth level to break out of, let's explore Level 5 and how many small wins can add up to something big.

CHAPTER 8

Level 5 ($10M–$100M)

Only the Paranoid Survive

The writer Jordan O'Connor noticed a pattern among the wealthiest self-made members of society—many of them didn't hit it big initially. It was their later projects that made them ultrawealthy. As he wrote:

> Many deca-millionaire, centi-millionaire, or billionaires have a story that starts with them selling their first company (in a very boring but reliable market) for $10M–$20M and netting at least a few million personally.
>
> Then it's just continuing to play the game with higher stakes, bigger markets, and bigger ideas.
>
> This first exit should be the first goal of aspirational entrepreneurs who want to tackle bigger things later in life. Not building a billion-dollar-company on their first try.[1]

The evidence supports this as well. Mark Cuban, of *Shark Tank* fame, among other things, sold his first company, Micro-Solutions, to CompuServe for $6 million in 1990 when he was thirty-two. He pocketed nearly $2 million after taxes.[2] Elon Musk sold his first company, Zip2, to Compaq for $307 million in 2002, seven years after it was founded. He netted $20 million from the sale.[3] Reed Hastings, the founder of Netflix, took his first company, Pure Software, public in 1995, and it was later acquired.[4] All these founders did well for themselves early on, but they didn't become the billionaires they are today from their first business endeavors.

Researchers at MIT's Sloan School of Management analyzed data on entrepreneurial success and concluded that this is the norm. Their research found a positive (and statistically significant) association between the number of companies previously sold by an entrepreneur in the past and their current company's total revenue. In other words, entrepreneurs with more prior exits had bigger companies today. For every additional company sold in an entrepreneur's past, their current company's revenues were 52 percent higher. This was after controlling for age, education, number of cofounders, and initial capital raised.[5]

Don't get me wrong, there are first-time founders who go on to create highly successful companies. Jeff Bezos with Amazon, Sara Blakely with Spanx, and Bill Gates with Microsoft are some examples that come to mind. However, the data suggests that these cases are the exception, not the rule. Cowboy Ventures, a venture capital firm, compiled a list of all the unicorn companies—those with a valuation greater than $1 billion— founded from 2003 to 2013. Among these unicorns, nearly 80 percent had at least one cofounder who had previously founded a company.[6] While the media likes to glorify first-time founders, most successful businesses have experienced leaders at the helm.

This insight is particularly relevant for those in Level 5, who likely already sold a business or currently own a business worth a lot of money. Either way, if you want to make it to Level 6, you have to decide between two options. Do you scale your existing business? Or do you create a new business with more upside potential?

Unfortunately, I can't answer this question for you. You'll need to decide for yourself based on your own motivations and your experience in your given industry. Either way, if you are unsure whether to scale your existing business, then that tells you something in and of itself. It reminds me of that famous story about Mozart and a young student. The student comes to Mozart one day and asks, "Mozart, I want to write a symphony. How should I start?" To which Mozart replies, "Given your age, maybe you should start with something simpler first, like a concerto." The student becomes visibly frustrated and says, "But you were composing symphonies when you were eight!" To which Mozart replies, "Yes, but I never had to ask anyone how to do it." There's nothing wrong with asking for advice, but sometimes the act of asking can provide the answer you are looking for.

If you decide to keep running your existing business, your primary goal should be to increase its value. And to do that, you almost certainly need to grow. This means more customers, more sales, and more profits. The reason why growth matters is that bigger companies tend to sell at a premium relative to many smaller companies put together. This really is a case where the whole is greater than the sum of its parts. For example, in the wealth management industry, ten firms with $1 million in annual revenue would be worth less than one firm with $10 million in annual revenue. There are two reasons for this.

First, larger firms can operate and scale more efficiently than smaller ones. That one larger wealth management firm doesn't need ten CEOs, ten chief compliance officers, and so forth. These economies of scale save money and lead to more profits, all else being equal.

Second, the earnings from the larger firm should be more stable than the earnings from the ten smaller firms. And since the larger firm's earnings are more predictable, they are worth more to potential investors. So even if the larger firm had the same revenue and profits as the ten smaller firms combined, most investors would pay more for the larger one than for the ten smaller firms as a group.

For example, if the larger firm had $10 million in revenue and $2 million in annual profit, it might sell for ten times its annual profit. In other words, it has a 10x valuation multiple. Assuming this were true, then the larger firm would be worth $20 million (10 * $2 million). But what about the smaller firms? If each one had $1 million in revenue and $200,000 in profit, they might only sell for an 8x multiple. This means that each of these smaller companies would be worth $1.6 million (8 * $200,000), and you could buy all ten of them for $16 million. While the larger firm and the ten smaller firms have the same annual revenue and profits, the larger one is worth $4 million more to investors.

Investors are willing to pay more for the larger firm because it is easier and less risky. The larger firm has one culture and one team ready to run the business. Combining the ten smaller firms into one bigger firm would be a nightmare. They have different cultures, likely use different systems, and it would require lots of work to integrate them. That's a major headache that you would have to deal with as an investor. This explains why larger firms have the valuation premium they do. Don't just take my word for it though. In *The Market Approach to Valuing Businesses,* Shannon Pratt states, "Smaller companies in most industries tend to sell at lower multiples of most financial variables than larger companies in the same industry."[7]

This is why your goal when running an existing business is to make it larger. Not only is the firm worth more when you have more profits, but you are also likely to get a bigger valuation multiple on those profits as well. Unfortunately, growing a business is incredibly difficult, which is why getting to Level 6 can be so elusive.

As much as I want you to scale your existing business into the next unicorn (i.e., a $1 billion company), unfortunately, the odds are against you. Cowboy Ventures found that less than 0.1 percent of all the start-ups in their database, or only about 1 in 1,500, ever made it to $1 billion in value.[8] This suggests that if you build a viable business and are offered a hefty sum for it, you should consider selling. Of course, there are many other factors to think about when making this decision. However, I've heard far more stories of people who regret not selling their businesses when they had the chance than of those who sold too early.

One of the reasons why selling your business can be so appealing is because it allows you to start fresh. Imagine all the mistakes you made in your first company. You probably wouldn't make those mistakes again if you started over. By selling your business, you'll have the opportunity to close one chapter of your life before embarking on the next. And when you start your next venture, there's a good chance it will grow even bigger than the one before, as data from the MIT study suggests.

Another reason to consider selling your business is the risk associated with not selling it. While having a lot of equity in an individual business can help create great wealth, it can also destroy it. There's nothing more disheartening than spending up to a decade on something and watching it decline due to bad luck. While a lot of things in the business environment are in your control, many of them aren't. Selling your business (or a portion of it) allows you to de-risk and stay in Level 5 rather than fall down the Wealth Ladder. Though concentration likely got you into Level 5, diversification will keep you there.

After all, outside of fraud, the most common way those in Level 5 (and above) fall down the Wealth Ladder is through overly concentrated investments. These investments can be in your own business or someone else's. Either way, the risk is in having too much money in a single asset. For example, Seán Quinn, who was once the richest man in Ireland, saw his wealth decline precipitously after some bad investments in an Irish bank. Björgólfur Guðmundsson experienced a similar fate after his large investment in an Icelandic bank forced him to file bankruptcy in 2008. Eike Batista, once the richest man in Brazil, lost most of his wealth after his oil company, OGX, went bankrupt.[9] Though each of these cases is unique, they all share one thing in common—overconcentration. Each of these people put all their eggs in one basket. They could easily have diversified and avoided such a fate, but they didn't. The same thing can happen to you in Levels 5–6 if you aren't careful.

Of course, the problem with telling someone who made it to Level 5 to diversify is that they probably won't listen. The characteristics that got someone to $10 million in wealth are likely the same ones that won't allow them to stop once they get there. If I had to guess, most successful business owners in Level 5 see themselves as temporary visitors on their way to Level 6. As the saying goes, "Every senator looks in the mirror and sees a president." I don't blame them for thinking this way. After all, building a business that generates $10 million in personal wealth is no easy task. However, I don't think the issue with those in Level 5 is their skills, but things outside their control. This is where diversification comes in handy.

Besides concentrated investments, you should also be wary of the other financial risks that you can experience in Level 5. This includes overspending, taxes, and other liabilities. If you got to Level 5 through a single liquidity event (e.g., a business sale), then it's possible that you don't know how to save money. You've never had to demonstrate financial discipline. This is especially true for those who skipped a wealth level after selling their business. And with all the new amenities available to those in Level 5, it can be easy to overspend if you aren't careful. If you recall from chapter 1, Level 5 is where you begin to have "House freedom" (i.e., you can live in almost any neighborhood you want). But buying your dream home is just the beginning. You also have to consider the upkeep on that home as well. This will include taxes, maintenance, and insurance. And the bigger the home, the larger these expenses tend to be.

My friend's parents sold their company and bought a property in the Seattle area for a little over $10 million. Their monthly maintenance and landscaping budget was over $3,000 a month! If we assume that they have another $10 million set aside for retirement, that means they could spend about $400,000 a year (i.e., 4 percent of $10 million). Therefore, the maintenance and landscaping on their property would eat up almost one tenth (~$36,000) of their annual retirement spending.

Factor in other expenses like luxury travel or having assistants on staff, and that $400,000 disappears more quickly than you might imagine. This is especially true in Levels 5–6, because the costs of higher-end experiences grow rapidly. As wealth manager Frazer Rice noted in *Wealth Actually: Intelligent Decision-Making for the 1%*, "The expense rises geometrically for relatively small gains in convenience and experience."[10] So unless you really care about these "relatively small gains" in convenience, be mindful of what liabilities you sign up for in Level 5.

Aside from your spending, taxes become an even more important line item in Levels 5–6. Having a good accountant and being mindful of your tax decisions (e.g., where you live, when you sell your assets, etc.) can make a huge difference to your bottom line. While taxes matter for everyone, the cost of tax mistakes increase tenfold with every new wealth level. This is especially true if you plan on leaving assets to your heirs after you're gone. Having the right estate plan can literally save you millions if the proper structures are put in place ahead of time. While it's hard to make general statements about taxes given how individualized they can be, having the right tax team should pay for itself in Level 5 and beyond.

What's true for your taxes is also true for your financial

life in general. Once you have $10 million or more, you will be presented with an endless list of "opportunities" for your wealth. Having a trusted group of experts that you can rely on to help you make big financial decisions is paramount if you want your wealth to last across generations. Your goal should be to have a *group* of people you consult with, so that no individual or single decision will lead to ruin.

The last thing to be mindful of in Level 5 is other liabilities. Make sure that you have an umbrella insurance policy that covers basically anything. Ensure that your property doesn't have any areas where someone could get injured. Do you have a dog that's a bit aggressive? Pay to get it trained. I can guarantee that if your dog bites someone, you will find yourself on the other side of an expensive lawsuit. I know these examples might seem silly, but it's the stuff you don't think about that gets you in trouble. This is especially true in Levels 5–6, because those things that wouldn't normally be a risk when you aren't rich become risks when you are. Unfortunately, as soon as someone knows you have lots of money, they can try to take advantage of you. I don't want you to go through life paranoid all the time, but as Andy Grove once wrote, "Only the paranoid survive."[11]

Risks aside, Level 5 is also where you should seriously consider whether continuing to climb is truly worth it. From a consumption standpoint, 99 percent of the world's experiences will be within your reach. There are very few things you can buy in Level 6 that you can't already afford in Level 5. So the real question is: Is striving for that final 1 percent worth the possible downsides? In this vein, let's explore why more isn't always better—and why you shouldn't let money define how you interact with the world.

Huguette Clark spent the last two decades of her life living in a hospital, although she wasn't sick. Her mansions in Connecticut and California sat empty, alongside her three luxury apartments on New York's Fifth Avenue. Other than her caretakers, Clark kept in touch with almost no friends or family. She lived the life of a recluse, shutting out the world.

But Clark wasn't always like this. She grew up in New York City as the daughter of William A. Clark, a U.S. senator and wealthy mining magnate. While in school, she had a vibrant social life. She would often attend parties with her friends or go to the opera with her mother. She periodically traveled across the country to visit her extended family in California. In her early twenties, Clark even got married, although she later divorced.

But after her parents' wealth came under her control, Clark's behavior changed. She began to ignore her extended family. She lost touch with her friends. She stopped going out and preferred to stay inside to make art. Ultimately, she stopped trusting everyone around her because she thought they just wanted her money. As her wealth grew, her relationships withered away. When she died in 2011 at age 104, she was worth an estimated $300 million. Not a single family member attended her funeral.[12]

While Huguette Clark was right to be skeptical of others' motives due to her vast fortune, she also let money define how she interacted with the world. Though her accommodations were materially better, because of money her life was invariably worse. While it's easy to see all the positive attributes that wealth can provide, the downsides are rarely discussed.

Anytime we talk about wealth there is an implicit assumption that more is always better. This is a foundational belief in modern economics. Economists call these monotonic preferences. This means that if I give you something you like, you will *always* prefer more of that thing over less of it. For example, if I know you like apples, then you should prefer two apples over one apple. Assuming that they don't cost you anything, two is better than one. After all, with more apples, you could eat them, sell them to someone else, or donate them to a local food bank. Either way, you can see why more is better.

Unfortunately, this idea doesn't hold when it comes to having more wealth. In general, more money is better than less money. Someone who is in Level 1 would almost always be better off if they were in Level 5 or 6. Getting people out of poverty is a good thing. However, I am not convinced that going past Level 4, for example, is always an upgrade. In fact, it could make a few areas of your life objectively worse. So let's take a look at some of the downsides of wealth that you may find in Level 5 and beyond.

Loss of Trust

One of the most difficult parts of acquiring wealth is the increased skepticism you may have around others. This is especially true if your financial status is known. Wealth can change your relationship with others because you don't know if they are interested in you or your money. Clay Cockrell, therapist to

the superrich, found that this was a common theme with many
of his clients:

> I hear this from my clients all the time: "What do they
> want from me?"; or "How are they going to manipulate
> me?"; or "They are probably only friends with me be-
> cause of my money."[13]

These feelings of distrust can influence how the rich choose
their friends, who they date, where they live, and much more.
Paul Hokemeyer, a clinical psychotherapist for the affluent,
told CNBC that wealthy people can come to be viewed as ob-
jects. He said, "Their relationships become defined for what
they can provide to others rather than for who they are of themselves."[14] Such a change in the relationship dynamics explains
why there can be a loss of trust in others in the first place.

It also explains why wealthy people tend to hang out with
other wealthy people. When Thomas C. Corley interviewed
177 self-made millionaires for his Rich Habits study, he found
that they tended to forge relationships with other rich and successful people.[15] This makes sense, as rich people know that
other rich people probably aren't trying to befriend them for
financial reasons. As a result, they can more easily form genu-
ine relationships based on shared values and interests.

Don't get me wrong, I'm not saying that once you reach a
certain wealth level that people will only like you for your
money. However, if your financial status is publicly known, you
will need to keep your guard up at times. This is why the
friends you had before you were wealthy are so important.

Because you know they liked you for who you are and not because of the wealth you have today.

While being slightly skeptical of others' motivations can be necessary if you have wealth, make sure not to take it too far. Huguette Clark is an example of someone who let money poison her relationships. Striking a balance between paranoia and prudence is the key to maintaining both your wealth and your relationships. But not all the downsides of wealth come from other people. Sometimes they come from within.

Increased Stress

Whether you are striving for more wealth or trying to protect what you already have, money can be a source of stress. This stress can impact your well-being and mental health, especially at higher wealth levels. For example, one study found that the relationship between wealth and mental health wasn't linear, but an inverted U shape. In other words, more wealth was associated with better mental health . . . to a point. However, beyond the peak, more wealth led to *decreased* mental health on average. This post-peak decline is what creates the upside-down U shape. The study's authors theorized that this inverted-U relationship occurred because wealthier individuals worked more and took more risk than their slightly less wealthy counterparts. As the authors of the study said, "To accumulate more wealth, some populations might overwork or invest in high-risk and high-return financial products."[16]

The evidence suggests that at some point more wealth stops having a positive impact on your life and can actually start to have a negative impact. William Vanderbilt, who was once the richest man in the world, echoed this sentiment when comparing his life to that of his less wealthy neighbor:

> He isn't worth a hundredth part as much as I am, but he has more of the real pleasures of life than I have. His house is as comfortable as mine, even if it didn't cost so much; his team is about as good as mine; his opera box is next to mine; his health is better than mine, and he will probably outlive me. And he can trust his friends.

Vanderbilt later said that being the richest person in the world brought him nothing but anxiety.[17] While we are unlikely to ever become the richest person in the world, you can imagine the stress and scrutiny created by large amounts of wealth. The responsibility one might feel toward society. The guilt of having so much while others have so little. These are the kinds of mental challenges you may face as you climb the Wealth Ladder. But even if you can deal with the increased stress associated with greater wealth, you may find that some of your problems are closer to home.

Altered Family Dynamics

The last thing you'll need to be mindful of while building your wealth is how that wealth impacts your family. This is especially true in Level 5 (and beyond), where resource division and fairness take center stage. For example, if you provide financial support to one of your adult children, how might your other adult children feel about it? If your sibling asks for money, would you help them out? What about distant relatives? Do you provide unconditional support or do you impose boundaries?

These are just some of the situations you may find yourself in when it comes to dealing with money and family. Managing this complex web of relationships while also instilling the right values in your loved ones can be hard to navigate.

For example, when it comes to your children, you may want to provide for them as much as possible. However, this may impact them in unexpected ways. One study by Suniya S. Luthar and Karen D'Avanzo found that children of affluent parents were more likely to use drugs and have mental health struggles compared with children living in the inner city. In a related study, Luthar noted:

> Affluent youth reported significantly higher levels of anxiety across several domains, and greater depression. They also reported significantly higher substance use than inner-city students, consistently indicating more frequent use of cigarettes, alcohol, marijuana, and other illicit drugs.[18]

When Luthar and D'Avanzo tried to determine why they were seeing such a result, they found that achievement pressures and isolation were to blame.[19]

Successful, wealthy individuals typically want their children to be successful too. However, such expectations can put enormous pressure on affluent youth to do well. To make matters worse, wealthy individuals tend to have more demanding careers that take time away from their families. As a result, children of the affluent are more likely to be physically and emotionally isolated from their parents. This leads to a paradoxical situation: While the wealthy work hard to provide their offspring with a better future, they may overlook those offspring in the present. Taken together, the isolation and achievement pressures experienced by affluent youth can contribute to an increased chance of mental health and substance-abuse issues.

To be clear, it seems to be the *combination* of isolation and achievement pressures that leads to this result and not just one or the other. For example, first-generation immigrants have been known to push their children to succeed; nevertheless, these children exhibit fewer substance-abuse issues than their native-born counterparts.[20] Motivating your children to excel isn't the problem. It's the context and the way in which you do it that matters.

On the flip side, wealth can also be demotivating for children who know that their parents will support them financially no matter what. After all, what's the point of pushing yourself if you know that Mommy and Daddy will always be there to write you a check? While wealth can provide great support to children in terms of education and life experiences, it can also remove any incentive to work hard. As the saying goes, "The silver spoon often chokes ambition."

Such scenarios can also lead to a sense of entitlement. If your children always get what they want from you, they may come to expect the same from the rest of the world. This sense of entitlement can make your children believe that they are better than others, that things come easily, or that the rules don't apply to them. All these beliefs can have negative consequences throughout their lives.

The solution to these problems is to strike a balance between providing support and promoting self-sufficiency. This will allow them to flourish without destroying their motivation or turning them into entitled brats. But where is the line between offering assistance and creating dependency with your children? No one knows for sure. Nevertheless, I am a fan of Warren Buffett's take on the issue: "Leave the children enough so that they can do anything, but not enough that they can do nothing."[21] While "enough" is open to interpretation, the ideal level of financial support should help your children thrive without jeopardizing their independence.

Outside your closest relatives, you may also run into awkward money situations with your extended family. If they know that you are doing well financially, they may expect you to pay for things or help them out if they ask. While I am generally supportive of these unspoken customs, there is a fine line between support and abuse. Paying for dinner on occasion is one thing, but becoming the personal piggy bank of the family is another. If you want to preserve the relationship, set some ground rules about when you are willing and unwilling to provide financial support. This may be difficult to discuss, but better to have an open dialogue than private resentment on either end.

Lastly, moving up the Wealth Ladder often requires sacrifices from you and from your loved ones. If you have a demanding job, this could lead to long hours and time away from your family. If you decide to start your own business, you might have to take on more financial risks. Your significant other may need to provide more support around the house. No matter how you decide to climb the Wealth Ladder, striving for more typically comes with costs. You need to set the right expectations with your family regarding these costs. Because if you don't, you may end up damaging your relationships and losing them as a result. Therefore, the goal with family should be to find the right balance between sacrificing for a better future and living in the present.

Though there is no perfect way to deal with these situations, effective communication is about as close as you can get. Communicating early and often about your values and your long-term plan for your family's wealth can help set right expectations with your loved ones. Ideally, you want to get everyone on the same page so that there are no surprises or feelings of resentment. Of course, effective communication is a two-way street. It also requires listening to those involved and making sure their voices are heard. If there is a difference of opinion, you should openly discuss it. Tell them why you feel differently and how you came to your conclusion. Then hear their side as well. You may not agree with what they say, but you should still listen to them and compromise where possible.

Obviously, these can be difficult conversations to have. Emotions can run high and feelings can get hurt. But as Alex Hormozi has been known to say, "The life you want is on the other side of a few hard conversations."[22] So if you want to prevent the kind of infighting over money that can tear families apart, then you should have these conversations before it's too late. The last thing you want is unresolved family tensions reappearing when you are no longer there to mediate them.

No matter how you decide to deal with money and your family, navigating this complex issue is no easy task. Trying to raise your children without spoiling them, ignoring them, and pressuring them is a challenge. Helping out your extended family without creating dependence can be difficult. Focusing on the future without sacrificing the present is a delicate balance. While I don't have the answer for every situation, your money should enhance your relationships, not threaten them.

Though your money is yours to control, if you want it to last, then you need to set proper expectations and get buy-in from your loved ones. While this isn't guaranteed to prevent 100 percent of all money fights, it should go a long way in helping preserve your family's wealth for generations to come.

Level 5 Summary

- **Follow-Up:** Decide whether to sell your existing business, start a new one, or stop climbing the Wealth Ladder altogether.

- **Opportunities:** Sell multiple businesses or scale an existing business.

- **Risks:** Concentrated business holdings. Overlooking personal liabilities. Increased stress, loss of trust, and altered family dynamics.

- **Mental framework:** Only the paranoid survive.

Navigating Level 5 successfully requires finding ways to scale and eventually sell your business. However, you'll have to do this while avoiding the many financial and nonfinancial risks that come up along the way. Unfortunately, both the financial and nonfinancial risks only get larger as you move up the Wealth Ladder. For this, we turn to our discussion of Level 6 ($100M+).

CHAPTER 9

Level 6 ($100M+)

Legacy = Action ⁎ Wealth

n 1888, a French newspaper published an obituary for Alfred Nobel that ran, "Dr. Alfred Nobel, who became rich by finding ways to kill more people than ever before, died yesterday."[1] There was just one problem—Alfred Nobel was still alive. The obituary was meant for Nobel's eldest brother, Ludvig, but had mistakenly been published about Alfred instead. The false announcement had a profound impact on how Nobel viewed himself. Years earlier, Nobel had invented dynamite as a safer alternative to nitroglycerin, a highly dangerous explosive, and got rich as a result. However, with his wealth came accusations that he was profiting from death and destruction.

As a result, Nobel was determined to change how he would be remembered. So on November 27, 1895, while in Paris, he signed his last will and testament in secret. A year later when he passed, the public eagerly waited to hear how Nobel's vast fortune would be distributed. To everyone's surprise, he left a relatively small sum to his family and friends, with the bulk of his wealth going to establish five prizes bearing his name. Though Nobel's family tried to contest his will and seize more of his fortune, they failed. When all was said and done, Nobel's estate was liquidated, and 31.5 million Swedish Kronor—or over $200 million in 2024 dollars—were placed into a fund.[2] The Nobel Prize had been born.

The story of Alfred Nobel highlights many of the issues associated with being in Level 6 of the Wealth Ladder. Nobel had to think about his legacy, about the responsibility of such great wealth, and about how his relationships would be impacted by it. I think this is a great place to start our discussion of Level 6, because it is the first wealth level where more money should be the least of your concerns.

Though there are some stark differences between having $100 million and $1 billion (or more), on a consumption basis they are quite similar. Once you enter the three-comma club, you can buy larger companies and make a bigger impact on the lives of others. There's no doubt about that. However, unless you want to own a private jet, a megayacht, or multiple luxury homes around the world, there are few things you can buy with $1 billion that you can't buy with $100 million. This is why your primary concern in Level 6 shouldn't be acquiring more wealth, but protecting what you have.

And to protect your wealth, you will need to guard against bad investments, overspending, and poor decision making. What I said about Level 5 is true for Level 6: You need to get a team of experts on your side. This will include financial, tax, and estate professionals. Without such experts in your corner, you could end up making a financial mistake that will cost you far more than the advice would have. These are some of the services that literally pay for themselves in Level 6. The reason you need them is because of the increased complexity of your financial life. As your wealth grows and becomes more difficult to manage, financial experts can add more value. This value comes in the form of making better decisions and fewer mistakes around money.

But protecting your wealth against bad investments and poor decision making is table stakes in Level 6. You'll also need to be aware of all the other ways your wealth can be destroyed over time. And, as in Level 5, many of them aren't necessarily financial. Let's look at each of these in turn.

Divorce

Of all the decisions you make in your life, who you decide to partner with may be the most important. Getting married is more than a romantic commitment; it's also a financial one. After all, if you choose the wrong partner, it could end up costing you half of what you're worth. And no matter how great your returns were, anything multiplied by 0.5 at the end isn't going to feel good. While divorce is damaging no matter where you are on the Wealth Ladder, the absolute costs are the highest for those in Level 6.

While I can't tell you how to pick the right partner, neglecting your spouse is a surefire way to jeopardize your relationship and your wealth. As Morgan Housel once wrote, "There are 13 divorces among the 10 richest men in the world. Seven of the top ten have been divorced at least once."[3] While I don't know what caused these divorces, I'm quite sure that working to become the wealthiest people on Earth didn't help.

So how can you prevent this from happening to you? Make sure you understand your partner and, more importantly, make sure you understand yourself. James J. Sexton, a prominent divorce lawyer, wrote in *How to Stay in Love*:

> I have learned, over and over, that marriages and other committed relationships fail for two fundamental reasons.
>
> 1. You don't know what you want.
> 2. You can't express what you want.[4]

Sexton, who has seen thousands of unhappy marriages end, says this from experience. This is why it is paramount that both you and your partner know and understand each other's needs. It's basically a requirement if you want a successful, long-term relationship.

Unfortunately, knowing both your and your partner's needs is easier in theory than in practice. First, many of us aren't sure what we want out of life, let alone our relationship. And, second, even if we know what we want, communicating that message clearly to our partner can be a challenge of its own.

If you fail to do this properly, the costs can be significant. And I don't just mean the financial costs, but the emotional costs as well. Separating from someone you've been with for a long time can be a big change. Sometimes these changes are necessary to get yourself to a better place, but it can still be extremely difficult. This is especially true when children are involved.

Nevertheless, if you want to avoid such an outcome, you have to do the work. There are no shortcuts to a happy relationship. Spending the time to understand yourself and your partner is an investment that will pay off in spades. This will be true both in your personal life and your financial life.

Lawsuits

As I touched on in Level 5, as your wealth grows you should be prepared to get sued more often. When people know you have money, some will actively try to come after you for it. And unfortunately, the court system is where you will likely end up. The second regrettable thing about a lawsuit is that it's rarely cheap. Lawyers are notoriously expensive, costing hundreds or thousands of dollars per hour. And if your case is more involved, you will need to hire a *team* of lawyers to defend yourself. Before you know it, you can easily have legal bills in the six-to-seven-figure range.

Because of the high costs associated with a lawsuit, you'll be heavily incentivized to settle. And the other side knows that. After all, would you rather pay $1 million in legal fees and win or pay $100,000 to your opponent and be done with the ordeal? While getting the moral victory can be important, sometimes it's easier to pay the fee and move on.

While I hope you never find yourself in such a situation, you should be prepared for it if you reach Level 6. Make sure you have a legal team you trust and ensure that your behavior minimizes the risk of such lawsuits. Never drink and drive. Make sure you have the right insurance policies in place. Protect your privacy. As I mentioned in the previous chapter, many things that wouldn't normally be risks become risks once you have enough money. Unfortunately, some of these risks end up manifesting themselves in a courtroom. Finding ways to guard against these *before* they happen is the key to preserving your wealth (and sanity) in Level 6.

Even if you are able to keep legal battles at bay, in Level 6 you may find that your changing motivations are harder to defend against.

Changed Motivations and Perceptions

One of the other downsides of getting wealthy is how you can be influenced to strive for more even when it isn't necessary. History is filled with plenty of examples of this, some of which ended tragically. One such story is of Roy Raymond, who founded Victoria's Secret alongside his wife, Gaye. Though Victoria's Secret started out successfully, it hit a rough patch in 1982. As a result, the Raymonds chose to sell their business for $1 million. That's about $3.3 million in 2024 dollars. At the time, they could've bought a ten-year U.S. Treasury bond and earned 13 percent a year risk-free for the next decade. In today's dollars, the Raymonds would've made over $400,000 per year in pretax interest income.

Instead, they decided to try their luck in business again and invested most of their money into their next venture. That venture was My Child's Destiny, a company that sold high-end children's products. Unfortunately, the concept didn't take off, and within two years, it filed for bankruptcy. To make matters worse, the Raymonds didn't incorporate My Child's Destiny properly and were left personally liable for their losses. Their homes in San Francisco and Lake Tahoe were seized along with some of their other assets. The stress from the bankruptcy ultimately caused the couple to divorce.

Despite these setbacks, Roy Raymond was still determined

to hit it big. Over the next few years, he tried founding a handful of other ventures, but none were successful. This series of business failures and mounting financial difficulties sent Raymond into a depression. In 1993, just three days after the IRS filed a lien against his earnings, Roy Raymond committed suicide by jumping off the Golden Gate Bridge.[5]

Though Roy Raymond never made it to Level 6, his story remains a cautionary tale of the dangers of striving for more when you're already wealthy. In 1982, there were 475,000 millionaires in the United States.[6] Roy Raymond was one of them. Given that the U.S. had a population of around 230 million people at the time, Raymond was in the top 0.2 percent of wealth holders. Yet that wasn't enough for him. While I don't know what drove Roy Raymond to strive for more, I do know that getting rich didn't stop him.

One of the problems with climbing the Wealth Ladder is that the higher you climb, the more wealthy people you meet. Some of them will be even wealthier than you. Maybe you meet them through a friend, an exclusive club you joined, or a new neighborhood you moved into. One way or another, you're going to run into wealthier people. And when you do, how do you think that's going to make you feel? Do you think that you'll feel good? I doubt it. Before you know it, you'll think you're less wealthy and less accomplished than you actually are. This concept is known as relative deprivation, and it has been studied for decades. The writer Misha Saul explains how relative deprivation tends to occur:

> The more of an outlier you are in *any* respect (money, intelligence, beauty, chess, archery, whatever), the larger

the gaps between you and the next best above and below. If you are of median wealth, well, so are many others (by definition). Good chance that in your milieu the differences are slight. [Sixty-eight percent] of folks live within one standard deviation of the mean, in that hill at the center of the bell curve. Now let's move to the right. The gaps between the richest and the best become enormous. . . . According to the latest *Forbes* list the difference in wealth between #1 and #100 is US$200bn. The difference between #100 and #200 is about US$7bn. There are literally hundreds of blokes with US$1.0bn flat. The closer you move to the average, the more crowded it is.[7]

In the world of wealth, these differences are the most magnified at the upper end. This is why someone who is only slightly more successful than you (by luck or by skill) may end up being much richer than you. As a result, you can feel like you need to catch up. Wealth can morph your perceptions past the point of necessity.

No one is immune from this either. Even the late Charlie Munger, Warren Buffett's longtime business partner, expressed regret about not having more wealth. Munger told Becky Quick in an interview a few weeks before his death in November 2023:

MUNGER: I'm not all that pleased. I could've done a lot better if I had been a little smarter, a little quicker.

QUICK: What are you talking about? You've had success in everything you've done in life. What would you like to do differently?

MUNGER: Well, no, but I might have had multiple trillions instead of multiple billions.

QUICK: Do you sit around thinking about this? What would you have done differently?

MUNGER: Yes, I do think about it. I think about it. Yes, I think about it, about what I nearly missed by being just not quite smart enough or hardworking enough.[8]

Munger is considered one of the greatest thinkers and most successful businessmen of his era, yet even he didn't think he had enough.

Wealth has an interesting way of distorting our perceptions and changing our motivations. Even people who are objectively successful can be made to feel otherwise. If you want to counteract these pernicious effects, then you will need to remember who you are and what you value. Finding ways to enjoy your money without identifying with it should be your end goal. That's how you protect your wealth from yourself.

Once you've done the work of protecting your wealth from financial and nonfinancial threats, the next step is to consider your legacy. After all, what's the point of being in Level 6 and having "Impact freedom" if you don't spend time thinking about your impact? It reminds me of that alleged Bob Marley quote: "Some people are so poor all they have is money." Don't be one of them.

Instead, consider the impact that you could have with your resources. What would you like to see changed about the world? Where do your passions lie? What's one problem you want to help solve? You might think that these problems are unsolvable, but they definitely aren't. Alfred Nobel was able to change the world for the better with a $200 million fortune. While you may not have the same resources as Nobel, your wealth could make a bigger impact than you think.

Consider the story of Jadav "Molai" Payeng. Payeng was an environmental activist from northeastern India who single-handedly replanted what became known as the Molai forest. His work started back in 1979, after he discovered a barren sandbar covered in dead wildlife. Determined to create a place where animals could thrive, he began planting bamboo trees by hand on the sandbar when he was just fifteen years old. His planting work continued for over three decades. By 2014, the once desolate sandbar was home to a forest exceeding thirteen hundred acres.[9] And it all happened because Payeng was determined to make a difference.

Jadav Payeng didn't have Level 6 wealth. He didn't have anything close to it. But what he did have was a desire to change the world around him. And he took massive action to make it happen.

Ultimately, our legacy is what we do. Our money simply amplifies it. If I had to write this as a formula, it would be:

$$Legacy = Action * Wealth$$

So what legacy do you want to leave behind and how will your resources contribute to it? It's a question that you can answer in any wealth level. However, it holds far more weight as you move up the Wealth Ladder.

> ## Level 6 Summary
>
> - **Follow-Up:** Protect what you have. Focus on the non-monetary aspects of life such as relationships, friendships, and health. These are all the things that money can't buy.
>
> - **Opportunities:** Consider your impact and legacy.
>
> - **Risks:** Divorce, lawsuits, changing motivations, undue risk-taking.
>
> - **Mental framework:** Legacy = Action * Wealth

———

Wealth can be a source of independence, joy, and freedom. However, it can also be a source of anxiety, division, and cynicism. What it means to you can vary based on how much you have. And, unfortunately, more isn't always better. So before you decide to venture further up the Wealth Ladder, ask yourself: Is it worth it? Will the ends justify the means?

Though money can be a tool for a greater life, it can also be a prison for a worse one. The lost trust. The lawsuits. The changed motivations and family dynamics. All of these can contribute to a life filled with anxiety that isn't worth the extra money. Of course, I can understand why you may be skeptical and lack sympathy for those who experience such issues. I might as well be telling you about these problems while playing the world's smallest violin.

However, I don't mention these "first-world problems"

because I want you to feel sorry for those with lots of money. No, I mention them so that you can avoid these pitfalls yourself. After all, what's the point of climbing the Wealth Ladder if your life gets worse as you move up it? This is why avoiding the downsides of wealth can be just as important as building wealth in the first place.

———

Now that we've finished exploring all the levels of the Wealth Ladder, let's turn our attention to how long it typically takes to climb up it.

CHAPTER 10

How Long Does It Take to Climb the Wealth Ladder?

C urt Richter, the American biologist, did an experiment in the 1950s that changed the way we think about hope and expectations. Richter placed rats in a small tank of water and recorded how long before they drowned. He found that the typical rat would swim for about fifteen minutes before giving up. However, Richter ran a variation on his experiment in which he would save a rat right before it drowned and give it time to rest before putting it back in the tank. He discovered that these "saved" rats ended up swimming for sixty hours, on average, before losing hope and drowning.[1]

Richter's experiment demonstrates how much our expectations can shape our behavior. If we think that something is impossible, like the drowning rats, we are likely to give up quickly. However, if we believe that progress is within reach, we can push ourselves further than we ever imagined.

When it comes to the Wealth Ladder, I believe that similar context is required. You need to have an idea about what's possible *before* you embark on your journey. Because without such context, you may give up far too soon. So how long does it take to climb the Wealth Ladder? Is it easier to get out of Level 1 than Level 2? And how many levels should you expect to climb within a few decades?

All these questions (and more) will be answered in this chapter. Because knowing which strategies to follow is only half the battle. Having the patience to see the results is the other. Without the ability to stick to your plan, none of the ideas in this book will prove useful. However, if you know how long it typically takes to move up the Wealth Ladder, then you can mentally prepare yourself for the journey ahead. Unfortunately, the mainstream financial media has tried brainwashing you to believe that it's normal to be wealthy in your twenties and thirties. Thankfully, we have data that proves otherwise.

To start, let's examine the typical household age in each level of the Wealth Ladder. We can do this by looking at the median (50th percentile) age of U.S. households across every level of the Wealth Ladder in the 2022 Survey of Consumer Finances.[2]

Wealth Level	50th Percentile Age
Level 1 (<$10k)	42
Level 2 ($10k–$100k)	44
Level 3 ($100k–$1M)	54
Level 4 ($1M–$10M)	62
Level 5 ($10M–$100M)	64
Level 6 ($100M+)	66

The first thing you might notice about this data is that the median age tends to increase as you move up the Wealth Ladder. This illustrates the impact that time has on wealth accumulation. Since older households have had more time to save and invest than younger households, we would expect them to have more wealth. And as the data suggests, they do. Another thing to note is that the median age in Level 1 is 42. Why is this so high? Because Level 1 is the default wealth level. It's where many of us start. Unfortunately, some people never make it out. Though age is positively correlated with wealth accumulation, this is only true on average.

The other thing this data does is bust a few myths about what the typical wealthy person is like. Unlike what the financial media likes to report, the typical household in Level 4 ($1M–$10M) isn't in their thirties or forties, they're sixty-two. This means that half of all millionaires are younger than this age and half are older.

But how much younger? We can figure this out by looking at the other percentiles of household age in each wealth level. For example, if we were to examine the 10th percentile age in each wealth level, we would know the age of the youngest 10 percent of households in that level. We can do the same thing for the 25th percentile age. I've done this in the table on page 148, which has the 10th and 25th percentile ages by wealth level, along with the 50th percentile age for context.

Wealth Level	10th Percentile Age	25th Percentile Age	50th Percentile Age
Level 1 (<$10k)	23	30	42
Level 2 ($10k–$100k)	26	32	44
Level 3 ($100k–$1M)	32	40	54
Level 4 ($1M–$10M)	43	51	62
Level 5 ($10M–$100M)	46	56	64
Level 6 ($100M+)	50	60	66

From this table we gain a far better understanding of how long it can take to climb the Wealth Ladder. For example, we can see that 10 percent of U.S. households in Level 4 ($1M–$10M) are forty-three or younger, and 25 percent are 51 or younger. In other words, less than one in four millionaire households in the U.S. are under fifty.

What is true in Level 4 is even more true in Levels 5–6, where households have far more wealth. Since accumulating this much wealth isn't easy, it makes sense why it would take longer to reach these levels. This explains why only one in ten U.S. households in Level 6 ($100M+) are fifty or younger.

But what about those who are truly exceptional when it comes to building wealth? What's the youngest age we see in each wealth level? We can use the 1st percentile age of U.S. households by wealth level to determine this.

Wealth Level	1st Percentile Age
Level 1 (<$10k)	19
Level 2 ($10k–$100k)	21
Level 3 ($100k–$1M)	23
Level 4 ($1M–$10M)	30
Level 5 ($10M–$100M)	32
Level 6 ($100M+)	36

These figures represent the age that the youngest 1 percent of households are within a given wealth level. Once again, this statistic is meaningless in Level 1 since Level 1 is the default wealth level. Age 19 in Level 1 merely reflects the youngest households surveyed in the data. The same thing is true to a lesser extent in Level 2 as well.

However, the 1st percentile age is far more relevant for the higher wealth levels. For example, 1 percent of households in Level 4 are thirty or younger. These households are outliers and represent the earliest age that one could ever hope to hit Level 4 in the United States. Yes, there are households that have hit Level 4 even earlier than thirty, but they would represent less than 1 percent of the households in Level 4.

So far, we've looked at the distribution of ages within wealth levels, but we should also consider how wealth is distributed by age too. If we don't, then we may only be picking up differences in the sizes of different age cohorts. For example, if there were more households in their sixties than in their thirties in this data, then our results would be biased *upward* in age. To control for this, we can analyze wealth level breakdown *within* each age cohort. The table below does this by providing the approximate percentage of U.S. households in each wealth level by age. Note that the percentages *in each row* add up to 100, representing all the households in a given age range.

Household Age	Level 1 (<$10k)	Level 2 ($10k–$100k)	Level 3 ($100k–$1M)	Level 4 ($1M–$10M)	Level 5 ($10M–$100M)
20–29	39%	36%	24%	1%	<1%
30–39	22%	28%	45%	5%	<1%
40–49	17%	22%	46%	14%	1%
50–59	15%	15%	46%	22%	2%
60–69	13%	17%	43%	25%	2%
70+	10%	15%	50%	23%	2%

As you can see, most of the wealth in the U.S. tends to be concentrated in Level 3. Yet this still varies based on age. For example, while 39 percent of U.S. households in their twenties are in Level 1, only 10 percent of households seventy and older are the same. Additionally, while one in four U.S. households in their sixties are in Level 4, only one in one hundred households in their twenties can say the same. This suggests that it's rare for older households to have little wealth, but even rarer for younger households to have lots of wealth. This doesn't mean that you are going to have to wait until you're seventy to see the fruits of your labor, but don't expect to see it in your twenties either.

Ultimately, this data demonstrates the importance of time when it comes to building wealth. It's easy to overlook this when you're making big changes in your financial life, but you must internalize it. After all, if the typical household in Level 4 and up is in their sixties, why would you expect to get there in your thirties or forties? Unless you take extreme action, you shouldn't expect extreme results. And there's nothing wrong with that. The goal of the Wealth Ladder isn't to climb it as quickly as possible or even reach the top, but to enjoy the journey.

But how long does this journey typically take? How many years are required to move up the Wealth Ladder? Although these are all good questions, we can't use the data we've seen so far to answer them. The data I've used throughout most of this book is the Survey of Consumer Finances (SCF) by the Federal Reserve Board. The SCF collects financial snapshots of U.S. households every three years. This is great for seeing how wealth is changing for U.S. households as a whole, but we can't say much about how any individual household's wealth is evolving over time. The problem is that each SCF snapshot uses a *different* set of households.

But if we wanted to truly understand how households build their wealth over time, we would need to follow *the same set of households* in each snapshot. This is known as "panel data," and it records information on the same set of subjects over multiple time periods. Thankfully, there is a data source that does this—the Panel Study of Income Dynamics. The PSID is one of the longest-running panel datasets on U.S. households and household wealth. Though the PSID started in 1968, the comprehensive wealth data began in 1984 and runs through 2021 (as of mid-2024). Because of this, we can follow the same set of households from 1984 to 2021 to see how they climbed the Wealth Ladder over time.[3]

To start, we will look at these households and how their wealth changed over a decade. To do this, I found the wealth level of every household in the PSID data and looked at their wealth level again ten years later for every year where data was available. I did this from 1984 to 1994, then from 1989 to 1999, and repeated this process for each decade with data through 2011 to 2021.

Once I had all these observations, I then calculated the percentage of households that changed from one wealth level to another across all ten-year periods. This included households that increased their wealth level, decreased their wealth level, or stayed in the same wealth level after ten years. This was all done in inflation-adjusted 2021 dollars, meaning that my results represent *real* changes in purchasing power over time, not just the decline of the U.S. dollar. Lastly, since the PSID wealth data goes from 1984 to 2021, I was able to analyze wealth changes through a variety of economic environments.

To this end, I have summarized this data and created the financial mobility table on page 153. Note that this table only includes households in Levels 1–5 because households in Level 6 are incredibly rare and not in the PSID data. To use this table, first pick a *starting* wealth level on the left side of the table and then an *ending* wealth level across the top of the table. Now find where these two intersect inside the table. That percentage represents the share of households in your *starting* wealth level that made it to your *ending* wealth level after a decade. For example, roughly 30 percent of households that started in Level 1 (<$10k) ended in Level 2 ($10k–$100k) after ten years. Around 18 percent of households that started in Level 3 ($100k–$1M) ended in Level 4 ($1M–$10M) after a decade. And so forth. The percentages in each row add up to 100, representing all the households starting in a given wealth level.

	Ending Wealth Level (after 10 years)				
		1	2	3	4	5
Starting Wealth Level	1	46%	30%	22%	2%	N/A
	2	17%	38%	44%	1%	N/A
	3	2.9%	7%	72%	18%	0.1%
	4	1%	1%	23%	72%	3%
	5	N/A	N/A	4%	41%	55%

There are a few notable things about this data. First, most households stay in *the same* wealth level over time. You can see this by looking across the diagonal of the table. For example, 46 percent of households in Level 1 are still in Level 1 a decade later, 38 percent of households in Level 2 stay in Level 2, and so forth. The diagonal has the highest percentage in every row except for Level 2, where you are more likely to end up in Level 3 after a decade. This suggests that the wealth level most people start in will most likely be the wealth level they end in a decade later.

Another notable thing about this data is that there is more mobility at the top and bottom of the Wealth Ladder than in the middle. For example, 72 percent of households in Level 3 tend to stay in Level 3 after ten years. The same is true for Level 4, where 72 percent of households remain after a decade. This suggests that once you get into Levels 3–4, it can be difficult to get out. However, this is less true for those households near the bottom or top of the Wealth Ladder, where there is more upward (and downward) mobility.

Speaking of downward mobility, one final thing to note is that the wealth levels with the most downward mobility are also closest to the top. Those households with the highest probability of going down a level over a decade are in Levels 4–5; 41 percent of households went from Level 5 to 4 over a decade, and 23 percent of households went from Level 4 to 3.

Now compare this to what happened to those households starting in Levels 2 or 3. Only 7 percent of Level 3 households fell to Level 2, and only 17 percent of Level 2 households fell to Level 1. This suggests that the mechanism that helps create great wealth can also destroy it. This makes sense, as the wealth of those in Levels 4–5 tends to be concentrated in investments, which can fluctuate in value. And when they fluctuate to the downside, a lower wealth level can result.

But what if we were to extend our time frame to twenty years? Would we see more wealth mobility among U.S. households? Yes. If we were to create the same table as above, except we extended our time horizon to twenty years, we would see the following:

	Ending Wealth Level (after 20 years)				
	1	2	3	4	5
Starting **Wealth** **Level** 1	34%	26%	37%	3%	N/A
2	12%	28%	55%	5%	N/A
3	3%	7%	61.8%	28%	0.2%
4	1%	2%	25%	64%	8%
5	N/A	N/A	10%	54%	36%

Compared to the ten-year table, the twenty-year results demonstrate far more upward mobility. In other words, households in Level 1 are more likely to be in Levels 3–4 after twenty years than ten years. Households in Level 2 are also more likely to be in Levels 3–4 after twenty years than ten years, and so on.

This makes sense, as these households have had an additional decade to build wealth and climb the Wealth Ladder. The only wealth level where this isn't true is Level 5. While the data on Level 5 households is somewhat limited, there's a valid reason why they may exhibit more downward mobility. Households in Level 5 tend to have a lot of their wealth concentrated in individual businesses (as we've previously discussed). As a result of this concentration, these households take more risk and are far more likely to see their wealth decline compared to those lower on the Wealth Ladder. This demonstrates some of the challenges associated with reaching higher wealth levels.

While these financial mobility estimates are useful regardless of what time horizon we examine, they aren't set in stone. What happened to a particular wealth level may not repeat in the same way. Instead, let's ignore the starting wealth level and simply ask: What will my future wealth level be? Will I be up a level, down a level, or in the same level after a certain amount of time?

I've summarized the mobility data on page 154 to answer these questions for both the ten-year and twenty-year time frames. The tables on page 156 reflect the same wealth level changes as the previous tables, but they do *not* control for the starting wealth level. Instead, they illustrate the percentage of U.S. households that shifted a given number of wealth levels over ten or twenty years.

Wealth Level Change (After 10 Years)	Percentage of U.S. Households
Down 2 Levels	2%
Down 1 Level	11%
No Change	63%
Up 1 Level	21%
Up 2 Levels	3%

As the table illustrates, over a decade you are most likely to stay within the same wealth level; 63 percent of all households experienced this outcome. The next most likely outcome was moving up one wealth level, which happened for 21 percent of households. This is nearly twice as high as the percentage of households that fell down one wealth level, at 11 percent. Lastly, only 5 percent of households in total moved up or down *two* wealth levels within a decade. This should give you a much better idea of what's possible when climbing the Wealth Ladder over a ten-year period.

If we were to do this same summary over a twenty-year period, we would see the following:

Wealth Level Change (After 20 Years)	Percentage of U.S. Households
Down 2 Levels	2%
Down 1 Level	10%
No Change	51%
Up 1 Level	32%
Up 2 Levels	5%

As mentioned earlier, there is far more upward wealth mobility when looking over a twenty-year time frame. For example, while 21 percent of households went up one wealth level within a decade, 32 percent of households went up one wealth level within two decades. Additionally, 5 percent of households managed to climb two wealth levels in twenty years, which is nearly double the percentage of households that accomplished the same within ten years.

Though all this talk of wealth levels is nice, how much of an actual change in wealth do these wealth level changes represent? Well, it depends on your starting wealth level. For example, of those households that went from Level 1 to Level 2 in twenty years, the average wealth gain was $52,352. Of those that went from Level 2 to Level 3, the average wealth gain was $273,341. And of those that went from Level 3 to Level 4, the average wealth gain was $1.67 million. This illustrates that going up one wealth level can mean very different things depending on where you start. As a reminder, these changes in wealth are also adjusted for inflation. I'm not just looking at household wealth in 2001 and again in 2021; I've adjusted the 2001 wealth for inflation. After doing so, you get the total wealth gains cited above.

More importantly, even if a household didn't move up a level on the Wealth Ladder, they still likely built wealth. For example, households that started in Level 2 and ended there twenty years later saw an average wealth gain of $7,960. For those that started and ended in Level 3, the average wealth gain was $154,771. And for those that started and ended in Level 4, the average wealth gain was nearly $1.1 million. This illustrates how many households continue to build wealth even if they don't technically move up a wealth level.

Overall, both the SCF and PSID data paint a somewhat positive picture of wealth mobility in the United States. Since there is a slight bias toward moving up the Wealth Ladder (as opposed to down it), this suggests that most households will build wealth over time. While the data comes from the richest country in the world during a prosperous period, there have been similar improvements in wealth across the globe. For example, a World Bank report found that the percentage of people living in extreme poverty (less than $1.90 a day) fell from 36 percent in 1990 to 10 percent by 2015. This translates to over 1 billion fewer people living in such conditions, despite a global population increase of over 2 billion over this period.[4] Though I don't have detailed data on global wealth mobility, the large declines in worldwide poverty suggest that more wealth is being built by more people than ever before.

Chapter 10 Summary

- Understanding how households built their wealth is important for setting realistic expectations for your own wealth-building journey.

- Older households tend to be wealthier than younger households since they've had more time to save and invest their money.

- The typical millionaire is not in their thirties or forties, but their sixties. The median age of those in Level 4 ($1M–$10M) is sixty-two.

- Over a twenty-year period, there is more upward wealth mobility than over a ten-year period. This reaffirms the importance of time on wealth accumulation.

- There's more wealth mobility at the top and bottom of the Wealth Ladder than in the middle.

- There is a slight bias toward moving up the Wealth Ladder over time both in the U.S. and around the world.

PART III

FINDING

YOUR

SUMMIT

A Note on Part III

Now that we've examined each level of the Wealth Ladder and how long it takes to climb it, we have a better idea of what lies ahead. Nevertheless, many of the issues highlighted on our tour of the Wealth Ladder are not unique to any particular level. Divorce can be equally damaging in Level 1 or Level 6. Lawsuits can be equally stressful. Families can be equally divided by financial disputes, no matter the amount.

However, certain facets of our lives are amplified by how much wealth we have. In Level 1, we saw how bad luck was amplified due to the lack of wealth. In Level 2, our career choices were amplified. In Levels 3–4, our investment decisions were amplified. And in Levels 5–6, our personal relationships were amplified.

Regardless of your wealth level, you should be mindful of all these things. They are all important for living a good life. However, their *relative* importance shifts As you move up the Wealth Ladder. The reason why is simple: as you gain more wealth, money solves fewer and fewer of your problems. Many of the issues faced by those in Level 1 can be solved with money. However, many of the issues faced by those in Level 6 can't.

This single realization has profound implications for those seeking to climb the Wealth Ladder. After all, what is the purpose of wealth? Will more money make you happier? And what are you climbing for? Answering these questions is reserved for the third and final section of this book.

So far, we've spent our time understanding the *financial* aspects of the Wealth Ladder. We've reviewed its risks. We've assessed its opportunities. We've even quantified how often people move up and down its levels. All of this has served one purpose: to climb the Wealth Ladder. But now it's time to zoom out and tackle a bigger question. While we can use the Wealth Ladder to live a richer life, can we use it to have a better one?

As we embark on this final leg of our journey, let's explore the age-old question of whether money truly buys happiness.

CHAPTER 11

Does Money
Buy Happiness?

D oes money buy happiness? It's one of the oldest and most-asked questions in human history. Yet the evidence is mixed. If you believe that money can't buy happiness, then you might have heard of the research that first popularized this claim.

In 2010, Nobel laureates Daniel Kahneman and Angus Deaton released a paper called "High Income Improves Evaluation of Life but Not Emotional Well-Being." Their paper found that while a higher income did indeed improve how people rated their life, it didn't have any significant impact on their emotional well-being after a certain income threshold. In other words, while more money could make you feel better about your life as a whole, it didn't make you any happier on a day-to-day basis once you earned over $75,000 a year.[1] This was the commonly accepted wisdom for over a decade. Money can buy happiness, but it levels off eventually.

However, in 2021 Matthew Killingsworth upended the world

of money and happiness research when he published a paper titled "Experienced Well-Being Rises with Income, Even Above $75,000 per Year." His paper found that both life satisfaction *and* emotional well-being continued to increase with income, even beyond $75,000.[2] This directly contradicted the findings of Kahneman and Deaton and created a problem for the happiness research community.

After all, if Killingsworth's paper disagreed with the work of two Nobel laureates, then who was right? Well, Kahneman and Killingsworth decided to team up and dig through their respective data to resolve the discrepancy. The result was a 2023 paper titled "Income and Emotional Well-Being: A Conflict Resolved."[3] Their joint paper identified two primary differences between Kahneman's and Killingsworth's research.

First, they found that Kahneman and Deaton's original measure of emotional well-being wasn't actually measuring happiness, but unhappiness. In other words, their paper couldn't differentiate between higher levels of happiness. For example, imagine I ask a bunch of people to rate how happy they are, from 1 to 10. Then I take that data and replace any value 7 or greater with just 7. All the 10s become 7s. All the 9s become 7s. And so forth. As you can imagine, we would no longer be able to differentiate between those who are extremely happy (i.e., the 10s) and those who are just mostly happy (i.e., the 7s). This is basically what happened in Kahneman and Deaton's original study. As a result, they weren't measuring whether happiness rose with higher incomes, but whether unhappiness declined with higher incomes.

These might seem like the same thing, but they're not. One is looking at whether more money can increase happiness. The other is looking at whether more money can prevent unhappiness. As Kahneman and Deaton found in their 2010 paper, it can't. No one is immune to unhappiness, no matter how much money they have. Therefore, the conclusion from Kahneman and Deaton's original paper would be more appropriately stated as "Unhappiness decreases with increasing income, but there is no further decline beyond ~$75,000."[4]

The second thing that Kahneman and Killingsworth found was that Killingsworth's data did show a leveling off of happiness as incomes rose above $75,000. However, this was only true for the unhappiest people. When Killingsworth looked at the bottom 15 percent of people in terms of overall happiness, those who earned above $75,000 weren't any happier than those making around $75,000. Once again, money is not an antidote for unhappiness.

Putting it all together, Killingsworth's research ultimately won out. Money can buy happiness, but not in every circumstance. Here's how I'd summarize what he found: If you are poor, more money will probably make you happier. If you are happy, more money will probably make you happier. But if you aren't poor and you aren't happy, more money won't do a thing.

Although "more money" refers to income (not wealth) in this context, we know that income and wealth are correlated (see chapter 2). As a result, we should assume that they are interchangeable when looking at money and happiness. Killingsworth's latest research seems to suggest this as well. His most recent paper found that those with a net worth between $3 million and $8 million (i.e., Level 4) were significantly happier than any of the income groups that he had previously studied.[5]

In other words, wealthier people tend to be even happier than initially imagined.

While there isn't a lot of happiness research on those with higher amounts of wealth, I can understand why wealth can lead to more happiness. I don't think it's the money itself that makes people happier, but what the money allows you to do. For example, I hate cleaning. I'm a tidy person, but I can't stand periodically dusting, vacuuming the floors, and so forth. So when I finally had enough wealth to justify paying for a cleaning service, I did. And guess what? It's worth every penny and I'm definitely happier because of it.

Having more money doesn't just allow you to spend more on yourself, you can spend more on others as well. Researchers have found that those who spent more of their income on others had greater happiness.[6] This result doesn't surprise me. However, it's also much easier to spend money on others when you have more money to spend in the first place. Money is like the oxygen mask on an airplane. You must first secure your own mask before you can assist others.

Though there is a strong correlation between money and happiness, I don't believe the relationship is directly causal. Having an extra zero on your bank balance isn't going to make you jump for joy every day. But having more wealth can transform your lifestyle and how you are able to impact others. That's where the additional happiness likely comes from.

In the context of the Wealth Ladder, more money will impact your happiness based on where you are today. For example, if you're in Level 1 or Level 2, more money is likely to make you happier. This is true whether we are discussing wealth or income. However, if you are in Level 3 or above, more money will probably only make you happier *if* you are already happy. If you are miserable in Levels 3–6, more money is unlikely to be the solution.

Even so, when we think about money and happiness, the relationship isn't a linear one, but a logarithmic one. This means that as your wealth increases, your happiness also increases, but at a decreasing rate. A chart showing how happiness changes with wealth might look something like the chart below:

At first, small increases in wealth lead to big jumps in happiness. However, as your wealth increases, you need even bigger jumps in wealth to get the same happiness boost. This explains why giving $10,000 to someone in Level 1 would impact them a lot more than giving the same $10,000 to someone in Level 6.

Happiness Based on Wealth

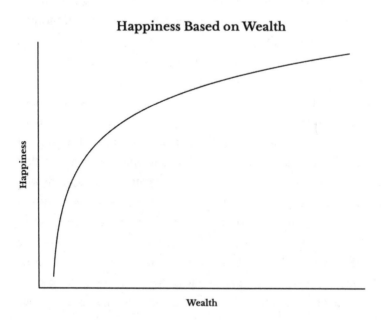

Unfortunately, the more money you have, the more you need to further increase your happiness.

This is the core insight of the Wealth Ladder and is backed by decades of research. *Axios* analyzed data from the Empower Financial Happiness survey and found that people with higher incomes needed to earn more than those with lower incomes to be happier. As they said, "Those earning more than $200,000 a year needed a salary of $350,000; while folks at the bottom of the income scale said $33,250 a year would do the trick."[7] This finding is nothing new. A 1987 poll conducted by the *Chicago Tribune* found that people who earned less than $30,000 a year said that $50,000 would fulfill their dreams, whereas those with yearly incomes of over $100,000 said they would need $250,000 to be satisfied.[8] It reminds me of that time when a reporter asked John D. Rockefeller, then the richest man in the world, "How much money is enough?" Rockefeller replied, "Just a little bit more."[9]

Regrettably, the yardstick we use to measure our life expands with our success. It's a moving target we can never catch up to. I've previously called this idea the "never-ending then."[10] Once I make this much money, *then* I will be satisfied. Once I have this much wealth, *then* I'll feel secure. Once I reach this wealth level, *then* I'll be happy. Unfortunately, this line of thinking is a mirage. Because once you reach a new milestone, you quickly get used to it. This idea is called habituation, and it explains why the happiness brought on by material rewards can be fleeting.

Many people try to solve this problem by striving for even more. But when you constantly chase your future, your future never comes. Every time you catch up with it, you end up pushing it further away. And given what we know about the Wealth Ladder, the jump to each successive wealth level becomes harder than the last. You end up constantly ascending and never satisfied.

The only way I know of escaping this loop is to shift your focus to the nonfinancial aspects of your life. These are the things that research shows can actually lead to more happiness than money. For example, one source of increased happiness is having more free time or leisure. Researchers analyzed data from seventy-nine different countries and found that "countries whose citizens value leisure more than work report higher subjective well-being at the country and individual level." This effect was found in both richer and poorer countries.[11] Then again, you can't enjoy your leisure time if you are constantly working to make ends meet.

Therefore, the ideal strategy for maximizing happiness seems to be to have enough money to alleviate struggle and worry, then focus on things *other* than money. As the saying goes, "Money can't buy happiness, but poverty can't buy anything." Escaping the poverty of Level 1 will almost certainly increase your happiness. But beyond that I'm not so sure. Don't just take my word for it though. Consider what Felix Dennis wrote in *How to Get Rich*:

> Still, let me repeat it one more time. Becoming rich does not guarantee happiness. In fact, it is almost certain to impose the opposite condition—if not from the stresses and strains of protecting wealth, then from the guilt that inevitably accompanies its arrival.[12]

Dennis's net worth at the time was estimated at nearly $750 million, which would put him comfortably in Level 6.[13] He knew what it was like to have money and the lifestyle that went along with it. Yet even he recognized the limits to wealth. When reflecting on whether he would do anything differently in his past, Dennis said:

> If I had my time again, knowing what I know today, I would dedicate myself to making just enough to live comfortably (say $60 to $80 million), as quickly as I could—hopefully by the time I was thirty-five years old. I would then cash out immediately and retire to write poetry and plant trees.[14]

In 2024 dollars, Dennis's ideal level of wealth was near the beginnings of Level 6. I doubt Dennis would need $60 to $80 million to write poetry and plant trees, but then again it depends on *where* you write poetry and plant trees. Either way, Dennis acknowledged the limited usefulness of money after a certain point. While that point is different for everyone, my guess is that it is lower for you than you probably think. Unfortunately, I don't have data to prove this, but I do have a story that illustrates it.

The happiest person I ever met was a facilities coordinator named Bud (not his real name). Bud helped maintain the office for the consulting firm I used to work for. Every day he would greet everyone he saw with a smile and a friendly gesture. He'd make small jokes and always try to lighten the mood. "And have a wonderful day!" was his signature line. He said it every time he exited a conversation with someone in the office.

I don't know how much Bud was paid and I don't really care.

But I do know that he wasn't paid the high six or seven figures that some of the firm's partners made in a good year. And while I won't speculate on the happiness of my former coworkers, I bet they would agree that they weren't as cheerful as Bud. They made multiples of his pay, yet had a fraction of his happiness.

I still think about Bud from time to time. He didn't have the title, the status, or the typical trappings of success. Yet he radiated joy wherever he went. He brought a smile to everyone's face. And it didn't cost him a thing to do it either.

Of course, I will never know if Bud's happiness was real or for show. After all, you can't know how someone truly feels on the inside. But if Bud was faking it, he faked it every day for the few years I worked with him. Rain or shine, he was there wishing us a wonderful day.

I know that my story about Bud isn't the same as a nationally representative dataset. It isn't on par with a randomized controlled trial or a best fit regression line. It isn't statistically significant. But there's something there. I saw it. I felt it.

If you think that money can't buy happiness, you're wrong. There is plenty of data that suggests otherwise. But if you think that more money will always lead to more happiness, you are also wrong. There are limits to what money can (and can't) do for your mental and emotional well-being. Thankfully, your happiness is more in your control than you might imagine. Bud taught me that, at the end of the day, our contentment boils down to our mindset more than what's in our bank account. What you take from his story is up to you.

Now that we've explored how wealth can influence our happiness, let's take a look at why wealth is the great enhancer of life.

CHAPTER 12

The Great Enhancer

When I first learned to cook, I thought salt was like any other ingredient in the spice rack. You add salt to food to give it more flavor just like you would add pepper, paprika, or chili powder. But I later learned that this was wrong. Salt isn't a spice like pepper, paprika, or chili powder. It's a mineral. Because of this, it has a different effect on food than a spice does. A spice adds a new flavor to your food. But salt doesn't. Rather, salt enhances the existing flavors. As Samin Nosrat wrote in *Salt, Fat, Acid, Heat*, "Salt has a greater impact on flavor than any other ingredient. . . . It enhances the flavor of *other* ingredients."[1] Salt makes our food taste more like itself. Without it, what we eat would taste bland. However, with it, the flavors of our food can come alive. In this way, salt is the great enhancer of the food world.

What salt can do to our food, money can do to our lives. Without money, life would be bland and limited. However, even a little bit of money can make life far more enjoyable. For example, if you enjoy listening to music with your friends, wouldn't going to a concert with them be even better? If you like watching tennis on television, wouldn't it be fun to attend the US Open? If you enjoy traveling domestically, wouldn't traveling internationally be a bigger thrill?

While money doesn't improve every experience, it can elevate a lot of them. But just like salt, there's a limit to this. Focusing too much on money can ruin other parts of your life, just like too much salt can ruin a perfectly good dish. Worst of all, money or salt by themselves aren't all that enjoyable. If you have money but you don't have friends, family, relationships, health, time, or purpose, what's the point? It's like having a plate full of salt, but nothing to eat it with.

The issue here is that both money and salt are only valuable relative to what's around them. So if you don't build a life with the *other* kinds of wealth that the world has to offer, then you will have climbed the Wealth Ladder for nothing.

Continuing with our analogy, so far we've tried to answer the question: How do I get more salt? But now we must shift our attention to an even bigger question: What should I be salting?

To do this, we must consider the other types of wealth that exist outside of money. What are these other types of wealth? I will refer to what the entrepreneur and creator Sahil Bloom argued are the five types of wealth:[2]

- Financial wealth
- Social wealth
- Mental wealth
- Physical wealth
- Time wealth

Since we've already covered financial wealth, let's take a look at these other kinds of wealth and how to think about them as you climb the Wealth Ladder.

Social Wealth

Of all the kinds of wealth you can have in this world, social wealth is one of the most important. Social wealth is based on the quality of your relationships. This includes your relationship with your partner, your family, your friends, your coworkers, and your broader community. The stronger these relationships are, the larger your social wealth.

More importantly, social wealth can enhance the other types of wealth in your life as well. For example, those with stronger relationships were happier and healthier as a result. As the authors of *The Social Brain* wrote:

> By far the biggest medical surprise of the past decade has been the extraordinary number of studies showing that the single best predictor of health and well-being is simply the number and quality of close friendships you have. By comparison, all the traditional factors that your doctor usually worries about on your behalf make only modest contributions.

Across 148 studies of 310,000 people, the best predictor of one-year survival following a heart attack wasn't how obese you were or how often you exercised, it was your friendships. In fact, the only thing that came close to having the same effect on one-year survival as friendship was giving up smoking.[3]

However, when it comes to friendship, more isn't always better. As researchers have found, the quality of your friendships seems to be more important than the quantity. According to a 2024 study published in the journal *Ageing & Society*, once you have four close friends, adding more did not have a "substantial beneficial effect" on reducing loneliness, depression, stress, or anxiety.[4] Though this study was conducted exclusively on older adults, it illustrates how a few close friends are better than many acquaintances. After all, if you have too many friends, your social attention could become too divided to build deep friendships in the first place. And these deep friendships are the ones that ultimately matter.

Social wealth is so important that you would need a lot more of other kinds of wealth to offset it. The neuroscientist Dr. Matthew Lieberman highlighted research showing how much additional income you would need to have the same well-being for various social activities. He found that:[5]

- Seeing a friend on most days was worth making an extra $100,000 per year.
- Being married was worth an additional $100,000.
- Seeing your neighbor regularly was worth $60,000.

While social wealth and financial wealth are not directly interchangeable, Lieberman's research illustrates just how valuable your social connections can be.

There is plenty of anecdotal evidence that relationships are one of the greatest joys in life. For example, Alfred Nobel, whose story we discussed in chapter 9, once wrote the following to his sister-in-law:

What a contrast between us! You live a warm and glow-ing life, surrounded by loved ones whom you care for and who care for you; you are anchored in contentment. I drift about without rudder or compass, a wreck on the sea of life; I have no memories to cheer me, no pleasant illusions of the future to comfort me, or about myself to satisfy my vanity. I have no family to furnish the only kind of survival that concerns us, no friends for the wholesome development of my affections, or enemies for my malice.[6]

Despite being one of the richest men in the world, Nobel couldn't buy the love and relationships that he so clearly val-ued. It's unfortunate to see someone so successful in one do-main completely fail in another. After all, what's the point of building wealth if you have no one to spend it with?

Despite the overwhelming research demonstrating the im-portance of relationships in our lives, many still find them dif-ficult to maintain. For example, research done by Lara B. Aknin and Gillian M. Sandstrom found that people were sur-prisingly hesitant to reach out to old friends. This was true even when "they wanted to, thought the friend would be apprecia-tive, had the friend's contact information, and were given time to draft and send a message." The authors theorized that this reluctance to reach out occurs because old friends can feel like strangers now. To test this hypothesis, the authors came up with a way to ease anxieties when talking to strangers. This intervention increased the number of participants who reached out to an old friend by two thirds.[7] While old friends can feel like strangers today, all it takes is one message to change that.

Of course, social wealth isn't just about who you interact with but who you don't interact with as well. The ability to remove negative people from your life can be just as powerful as the addition of positive people. As the American filmmaker John Waters once said, "I'm rich! I don't mean money-wise. I mean that I have figured out how to never be around assholes at any time in my personal and professional life. That's rich." In other words, real wealth is never having to spend time with assholes.[8] Leaving a toxic relationship or changing jobs due to a bad boss will improve your life more than you might initially imagine. Negative relationships are like the flu. You forget they exist when they don't impact you, yet they are all-consuming when they do. Finding ways to exit such relationships will work wonders for your well-being.

Additionally, when it comes to the intersection of social wealth and financial wealth, those with more financial wealth tend to have an easier time in their relationships. Having money reduces stress and relationship frictions while also allowing you to focus on the other problems in your life. This is especially true in romantic relationships. While financial wealth isn't necessary for a successful romance, having financial stability definitely helps. Results from a 2024 Forbes Advisor survey confirmed this. When researchers asked whether financial stability was necessary for a happy and successful relationship, 89 percent of respondents agreed.[9]

The empirical evidence agrees with this as well. Couples with more financial wealth were less likely to get divorced than couples with less financial wealth. According to a 2023 study published in the journal *Demography*, "Having $40,000 in wealth rather than $0 is associated with as big a decline in average predicted divorce risk as having $400,000 rather than $40,000."[10] In other words, going from Level 1 to Level 2 provides as large a decline in divorce risk as going from Level 2 to Level 3. While I don't expect this pattern to continue all the way up the Wealth Ladder, it illustrates how having some financial wealth can enhance your social wealth. Of course, this has its limits. As I discussed in Levels 5–6, too much financial wealth can have social downsides. Let's just hope you never experience them.

While your relationships with other people will be incredibly important for your well-being, your relationship with yourself can't be ignored either. For this, we turn to mental wealth.

Mental Wealth

Mental wealth is the extent of your psychological and emotional capabilities. It's your mental *health* and then some. Are you often stressed? How would you rate your self-esteem? Do you enjoy the work you do? All of these are related to your mental wealth and how you experience the world on a day-to-day basis. Though there are many different components of mental wealth, let's focus on work, stress, and self-esteem. If you can improve these three areas of your life, your mental wealth will grow considerably.

As the saying goes, "Do what you love and you'll never have to work a day in your life."

Work can be one of the most fulfilling and important aspects of existence. It's how we support ourselves. It's how we support our loved ones. And, for many of us, it's a crucial part of our identity. Work is how we relate to the world and how we fit into society. It can also provide a sense of achievement, purpose, and community. According to a 2021 report by the Pew Research Center, work was one of the biggest sources of meaning for people across seventeen advanced countries.[11]

If you don't feel this way about your work now, that's fine. But your goal should be to get there eventually. Because while it's easy to see work as something that we must do to survive, it can also be so much more. As Dorothy Sayers wrote in her essay "Why Work?":

> I asked that [work] should be looked upon, not as a necessary drudgery to be undergone for the purpose of making money, but as a way of life in which the nature of man should find its proper exercise and delight and so fulfill itself.[12]

This is how work can contribute to increased mental wealth. While early retirement and being disengaged at work (i.e., quiet quitting) are currently all the rage, I ask that you reconsider such notions. The goal of work shouldn't be to do less while getting paid more or to do nothing at all. The goal of work should be to find meaning in what you do. Because when you get paid to contribute very little, you end up giving up one of the most important things in your life—your purpose. Former President Richard Nixon summarized this idea beautifully in an interview from 1977:

> The unhappiest people of the world are those in the international watering places like the south coast of France, and Newport, and Palm Springs, and Palm Beach. Go-

ing to parties every night. Playing golf every afternoon, then bridge. Drinking too much. Talking too much. Thinking too little. Retired. No purpose. As so, while I know there are those who would totally disagree with this and say, 'Gee, if I could just be a millionaire that would be the most wonderful thing. If I could just not have to work every day. If I could just be out fishing or hunting or playing golf or traveling, that would be the most wonderful life in the world,' they don't know life. Because what makes life mean something is purpose. A goal. The battle. The struggle. Even if you don't win it."[13]

Nixon understood the importance of work and the positive impact it can have on your life. Of course, this doesn't mean that you should never retire, only that you shouldn't discount the benefit of having something to do. As Ernie Zelinski stated in *How to Retire Happy, Wild, and Free*, "Those who can retire from their primary career, but then find some sort of other work, are the happiest and suffer the least depression."[14] So if you want high mental wealth throughout your life, don't avoid work, embrace it.

While your vocation can be a source of joy in your life, it can also be a source of stress. Stress is a physiological response to a challenging situation. It's completely natural and shouldn't be feared or avoided. However, when you turn on your stress response too often, it can become a problem. As Robert Sapolsky wrote in *Why Zebras Don't Get Ulcers*:

When we sit around and worry about stressful things, we turn on the same physiological responses—but they are potentially a disaster when provoked chronically. A large body of evidence suggests that stress-related disease emerges, predominantly, out of the fact that we so often activate a physiological system that has evolved for responding to acute physical emergencies, but we turn it on for months on end, worrying about mortgages, relationships, and promotions.[15]

If you find yourself chronically worried in life, finding ways to destress will be paramount for keeping your mental wealth intact. Studies show that exercise, sleep, meditation, yoga, as well as various mindfulness techniques can help to reduce stress.[16] Whatever you decide to do, finding what works for you is what's important.

Lastly, focusing on yourself and your self-esteem is another key component of mental wealth. And for many, self-esteem is built on how they perceive their social status. If you believe that you haven't accomplished anything, then you will probably feel low status. But if you believe that what you do has purpose, then you will feel high status.

More importantly, your perceived status does not need to be based on money or career accomplishments. You can find status and self-esteem in many areas of life. Once again from Robert Sapolsky:

So, the lowly subordinate in the mailroom of the big corporation may, after hours, be deriving tremendous prestige and self-esteem from being the deacon of his church, or the captain of her weekend softball team, or may be the top of the class at adult-extension school.

One person's highly empowering dominance hierarchy may be a mere 9-to-5 irrelevancy to the person in the next cubicle.[17]

Status is *relative* to the context in which it is being evaluated. For example, if you are a competitive powerlifter, your status is determined by how much you can lift (strength) and how many competitions you have won (competitiveness). If you are a venture capitalist, your status is determined by what companies you have invested in (network) and how well those companies have performed (money). In other words, VCs don't care how much you can bench and weight lifters don't care about your investment returns. Both groups have their own standards for judging members of their community, and they care much less about everything else.

Thankfully, you get to choose which status game you want to play and how you want to evaluate yourself. This is both a blessing and a curse, because you can be objectively great at something and feel like a failure or you can be just okay at something and feel like a massive success. It's all based on how you feel. It's based on the story you tell yourself about yourself.

This brings us to the intersection of mental wealth and the Wealth Ladder. As I've discussed before, getting out of Level 1 will work wonders toward building your mental wealth. Not only will you be less stressed, but you should be able to find better work and feel better about yourself. However, beyond Level 1 there are no guarantees.

Money can't buy meaning or self-esteem. There are scores of depressed wealthy people who prove this point. Accomplishing something that is related to money can boost your mental wealth, but it's not the money that matters, it's what you accomplished. Just go ask a lottery winner or a trust fund baby how "successful" they feel and you'll see what I mean. You can't find mental wealth in a bank balance.

While how you treat your mind will be crucial to living a good life, how your treat your body may be even more important. For this we turn to our next section.

Physical Wealth

The Roman poet Virgil once wrote, "The greatest wealth is health." Over two thousand years later, the rapper Pusha T said, "Ask Steve Jobs, wealth don't buy health." The timelessness of such advice illustrates the predominance of physical wealth over the other kinds of wealth in our lives. If you don't have physical wealth, none of the other types of wealth ultimately matter. This isn't just an opinion either; there's data to back it.

If you recall from the section on social wealth, I highlighted research on the additional income needed to have the same well-being as regularly seeing a friend or neighbor. Well, according to that same study, being in good physical health was worth an additional $400,000 a year in salary. This was four times larger than any other metric analyzed. As the study concluded, health was by far "the most valuable nonmonetary asset researchers examined."[18] If you've ever been sick or injured, then you know how debilitating not feeling healthy can be. One day you are enjoying life and the next you can't enjoy much of anything. Anytime I'm like this all I can think of is what I would give up just to feel better again. This is why our physical wealth is so important for all the other kinds of wealth out there.

But what can we do to improve it? The evidence points to four key pillars of physical wealth: sleep, nutrition, strength, and cardiorespiratory fitness. I don't need to tell you to get more sleep and to eat healthier. Everyone has heard this advice before. However, what you may not know is the overwhelming importance of strength and stamina for your physical wealth. For example, in a study of active male firefighters, those who were able to complete more than forty push-ups had a 96 percent reduction in incident cardiovascular disease events compared with those who could complete fewer than ten push-ups.[19] In other words, stronger firefighters had fewer heart attacks.

This finding wasn't isolated to men either. If anything, women benefit *even more* from strength training than men do. Research published in 2024 in the *Journal of the American College of Cardiology* concluded that "Women compared with men derived greater gains in all-cause and cardiovascular mortality risk reduction from equivalent doses of leisure-time physical activity." Though their conclusion was for physical activity as a whole, the activity associated with the greatest reduction in mortality risk for women was 2–3 muscle-strengthening sessions per week. This result is partially due to the fact that fewer women do strength training. Out of the roughly 225,000 women in their study, only 20 percent participated in weekly strength training sessions.[20] This is even more reason for women to include strength training in their exercise program.

While the benefits of strength training are clear, the data on cardiorespiratory fitness may be even more compelling. A common way that researchers evaluate cardiorespiratory fitness is through VO2 max, a measure of the maximum rate of oxygen consumption during physical activity. Peter Attia discussed the importance of VO2 max on the *Huberman Lab* podcast in August 2022:

> If you compare the bottom 25 percent to the top 2.5 percent . . . the bottom quarter to the elite, for a given age, you are talking about . . . [a] 400 percent difference in all-cause mortality.

In other words, having a VO2 max in the top 2.5 percent for your age and sex drops your risk of death by 80 percent! Attia went on to say, "That's probably the single strongest association I've seen for any modifiable behavior."[21] Of course, you don't need a top 2.5 percent VO2 max to see a significant health benefit. Even going from the bottom 25% percent to the 50th–75th percentile (i.e., slightly above average) reduces your risk of death by 50 percent. For context, a nonsmoker only has a 29 percent lower chance of death compared to a smoker. If that doesn't illustrate the importance of doing occasional cardio to get your blood pumping, then I don't know what will.

In terms of physical wealth and the Wealth Ladder, there is evidence that people with more money tend to be healthier. For example, the famed Whitehall study found that even when you control for smoking, level of exercise, and other factors, lower socioeconomic status was still associated with higher cardiovascular mortality.[22] However, more recent research suggests that it's not the difference in money that is driving this result, but the difference in social rank. Since social rank tends to be highly correlated with income and wealth, it's this rank that is impacting health, not the money. As the authors wrote, "When evaluated simultaneously the ranked position of income/wealth but not absolute income/wealth predicted all health outcomes."[23] In other words, you should experience better health in a high-ranking, low-paid position than in a low-ranking, highly paid one. The example that immediately comes to mind is being an analyst at an investment bank. Though the job is well paid, it is notoriously stressful because analysts are at the bottom of the investment banking totem pole. This research suggests that you would be far better off with more status and less money than the other way around.

In full, while money can impact your physical wealth, other factors are likely to be more important. One such factor is the resource that we can't buy more of—time.

Time Wealth

Time wealth is the ability to spend your time how you want. Unfortunately, most people are limited in their time wealth because they have to work in order to survive. They can't do what they want when they want, otherwise they wouldn't be able to afford food and shelter. This has been the default way of living for most people throughout the ages. Historically, our very existence required our time.

However, over the last century we've seen a rise in leisure unlike ever before. According to research published in the *Journal of Political Economy Macroeconomics*, "Nowadays, American workers spend on average 2,000 hours a year at work, while their 1900 counterparts worked 50% more." This isn't just an American phenomenon either. Hours per worker declined in basically all of the forty-two OECD countries analyzed. The researchers attributed this change to both the increase in wages and the 50 percent decline in the real price of recreational goods and services since 1900.[24] In other words, we work less because people make more money and entertainment has gotten cheaper. And with less work comes increased time wealth.

However, more time wealth isn't always better. While being able to do what you want all the time might seem attractive on the surface, if you don't know what you want to do with your time, it can lead to an existential crisis. This is a common problem experienced by recent retirees who built their lives around their careers. John Osborne, a retired educational psychology professor who teaches a course on how to retire happy, echoed this sentiment in Ernie Zelinski's *How to Retire Happy, Wild, and Free*:

> The more your life revolves around work, the more of a shock retirement will be. It's like having a portfolio that's not diversified, and it's not until your job is gone that you confront reality. It can be like falling into space.[25]

That "falling into space" feeling is what can happen when your time wealth suddenly increases without you knowing how you want to spend it.

While it can be tempting to glorify such free time, time spent with purpose is far more valuable. I'd rather have one hour a day doing something I get immense value from than ten hours a day in mindless leisure. So before you yearn for more time, make sure you are properly spending what you already have. It reminds me of a quote from Seneca in "On the Shortness of Life":

It's not that we have a short time to live, but we waste a lot of it. Life is long enough, and a sufficiently generous amount has been given to us for the highest achievements if it were all well invested.[26]

Of course, the ability to spend purposeful time is a luxury that requires some financial wealth. You don't have to be too far up the Wealth Ladder to do this, but you will definitely need to escape Level 1. Once you are out of Level 1, then you can start focusing on work and leisure activities that are more meaningful to you.

This is why the true measure of time wealth isn't how much free time you have, but how much of that you are spending in activities that you find valuable. You can spend that time with friends and family, on your mental and physical health, or accomplishing something in your career. Whatever you decide to do, be intentional with your time. Because it's the only kind of wealth that you will never get more of.

———

There are many types of wealth that the world has to offer. Finding the right balance among them is essential for a fulfilled life. Unfortunately, you can't maximize every kind of wealth at once. When you go to chase one type, you typically draw resources away from the others. It reminds me of that joke about college: "You can have good grades, a vibrant social life, and great sleep, but you can only pick two."

While we don't actually have to pick one form of wealth over another, we do get to decide how we feel about the wealth we already have. Because there's a big difference between *being* wealthy and *feeling* wealthy. Even if you are wealthy on paper, if you don't believe it, then it doesn't matter. You could have $10 million, but if you feel like you need $20 million, then you will always feel poorer than someone with $100,000 who only feels like they need $50,000. A wealthy life isn't a number, it's a feeling. And where you derive that feeling from is up to you.

Ultimately, your financial wealth is a multiplier of every other kind of wealth you have. So if you don't have any other kinds of wealth, then your money won't make any difference. After all, any number multiplied by zero is still zero. You must be mindful of the other types of wealth in your life. That's how you ensure that your journey up the Wealth Ladder will have been worth it.

With that being said, let me tell you about my own journey up the Wealth Ladder.

CHAPTER 13

My Journey up the Wealth Ladder

M y parents met while working at McDonald's in the late 1980s. She ran the drive-thru and he worked the grill. They both came from working-class families. My grandmothers were stay-at-home parents and my grandfathers were manual laborers. One was a cement mason and the other worked at a grocery store. None of them were college educated. My parents would both attend community college, but would eventually drop out. They got married, had me and my sister, and then bought a condo in a working-class suburb. But it wouldn't last.

When I was six years old, they declared bankruptcy, divorced, and then my father moved in with his brother. I would see him every other weekend for the next twelve years. Both of my parents eventually remarried, and my sister and I learned how to deal with stepfamilies.

Growing up, money was somewhat scarce, but I never went hungry as a child. Most of the food I ate was either cooked at home or from the value menu (i.e., the $1 menu) at a fast-food chain. Going out to a restaurant was reserved for special occasions or when my grandparents covered the bill.

I only have a few childhood memories where money, or the lack of it, had an impact on me. One is my mother buying off-brand products at the grocery store to save money when I was little. She'd buy the fake Oreos or the non-Jif peanut butter as if I wouldn't notice the difference in taste. I always did. Another time is when my parents couldn't afford to pay the internet bill. It happened once or twice while I was in middle school, but those few weeks without internet were a challenge. All my friends were chatting on AOL Instant Messenger (AIM) and I wasn't. This was before cell phones and text messaging were around, so not being on the internet was crippling to your social life. Lastly, I never had my own car in high school. I got used to asking friends for a ride or borrowing my parents' car on the rare occasion they weren't using it. In the grand scheme of things, none of these were major issues, but I remember them nonetheless.

I didn't really start to understand money on a deeper level until I went to college. I was fortunate enough to get into Stanford University right as they rolled out a very generous financial aid policy. If your parents' income was less than $100,000, you didn't have to pay tuition, and if it was less than $60,000, you didn't have to pay room and board. For four years I didn't have to pay any tuition and for three of those four years I didn't pay room and board either. I just happened to be at the right place at the right time.

Despite this, Stanford exposed me to different lifestyles and upbringings, many of which were impacted by money. Some of these differences were relatively insignificant. For example, many of my classmates had been to Europe, but I hadn't. When my roommates discussed the quirkiness of their SAT tutors, I couldn't relate because I'd never had one.

There were also things related to class and etiquette. I'll never forget the first time eating out with all my freshman hallmates at a restaurant. As the entrées started coming out, I noticed that no one was touching their food. Anytime I was with my family, I always started eating as soon as my food came because it would be hot. But as I discovered that night, eating before everyone else had their entrée was considered rude. So when my plate came, I didn't do a thing. Then, as soon as the last entrée hit the table, it was as if a starting gun had been fired. Everyone started eating.

But there were some differences that were a bit more significant. Like knowing what to do when it came to applying for internships and navigating the job market. My friend Michael changed my life when he asked me, "Which summer internships are you applying to?" It was the winter of my sophomore year and apparently recruiting had already started for that summer's internships. As Michael explained to me, a sophomore year internship was very important. Having a sophomore year internship made it much easier to get a junior year internship the following year. And if you got a junior year internship and didn't screw it up, then you basically guaranteed yourself a full-time job offer after graduation. A decision I was supposed to make in the winter of my sophomore year would end up affecting my whole life. There was just one problem—I was oblivious to all this before Michael told me. I had never put together a résumé before, and many of the internship deadlines had already passed. I threw something together overnight based on my limited experience, but it didn't matter. I got rejected everywhere I applied.

While I considered this a failure at the time, that simple conversation with Michael got me into résumé-building mode. I spent the next year and a half focused on making mine better. I took on a few roles as a research assistant, which helped me secure a legitimate internship during my junior year summer. That internship allowed me to secure a full-time job offer, and eventually, the job that would start my career.

Looking back on my life before graduating college, I couldn't tell you which wealth level I was in at any given point in time. My parents bankruptcy when I was six years old, by definition, would have put us in Level 1 (<$10k). However, my parents always had family they could rely on if they needed money. They also both owned real estate at different points in time. This would easily have put us in Level 2 for most of my childhood.

I also would have considered myself in Level 2 right after I left college. Though I only had $1,000 to my name shortly after my graduation in 2012, I never experienced what it was like to be in Level 1. Like Mike Black from Million Dollar Comeback, I had many assets that you wouldn't find on a balance sheet, one of them being my high-end, private-school education.

As a result of that education, I earned a good income right out of school and was able to save money. Within a year my net worth surpassed $10,000. I was officially Level 2 before I knew what Level 2 was. But I also knew the importance of starting early, so I kept pushing. My goal back then was to get to $100,000, because Charlie Munger emphasized the importance of getting your first $100,000. As he said, "I don't care what you have to do—if it means walking everywhere and not eating anything that wasn't purchased with a coupon, find a way to get your hands on $100,000."[1]

While I wasn't buying food with coupons or walking everywhere, I went into overdrive to get to $100,000. At the time, I worked at a litigation consulting firm where we had cases and had to keep track of how much we worked on each case. I also knew that our bonuses were partially determined by the number of hours we worked. As a result, I started working more. I took every case that came my way and tried to help out other teams wherever I could. Before I knew it, I had a full caseload and was regularly working fifty to sixty hours a week. It wasn't easy, but I was in my early twenties and knew I had the energy to do it. More importantly, I was gaining valuable skills along the way. I learned data analytics and how to code in various programming languages. I got experience working in teams and managing people. I also became a much better communicator and writer.

All that hard work started to pay off too. As my income grew through my bonuses, I invested those extra dollars into index funds and ETFs. I was mostly buying global stocks and U.S. bonds back then, but later expanded into other income-producing assets. My money was making money, and it was a great feeling.

This strategy worked . . . for a while. Though my bonuses grew initially, I quickly maxed out my compensation. Before I knew it, I had hit a point where I couldn't earn much more without getting a higher-level degree like an MBA or a PhD.

That wouldn't have bothered me normally, but I wasn't in love with the job. Though I enjoyed working with data, I had no passion for litigation consulting.

As a result, I knew I had to make a change. So in 2017, I decided to start writing about what I did enjoy—personal finance and investing. I created a website called Of Dollars And Data (OfDollarsAndData.com) and began posting once a week. The first year was tough. I experienced a difficult breakup, I was no longer enjoying my litigation consulting job, and I had no idea whether my writing would ever take off.

Every week I spent ten hours writing a blog post and felt like I was going nowhere. I had a constant fear of failure. It was so bad that I originally started my blog anonymously in case it didn't work out. I cannot tell you how many times I thought about giving up.

There's something they don't tell you about being a new blogger on the internet. When people don't like your work, they don't tell you that it sucks. No, when people don't like your work, they don't tell you anything at all. For a blogger, rejection isn't hate, it's silence. Cold, hard, uncaring silence. And that silence is deafening. As the late Elie Wiesel was known to say, "The opposite of love is not hate, but indifference." Anyone who has ever created content knows this well. They begin to understand the depths of rejection.

Because when people typically talk about rejection, it is almost always in the context of dating. However, that rejection is trivial compared to the form of rejection you get when you are producing content publicly, for the world to see.

When you're turned down by a potential partner, countless reasons could be at play: They might not find you physically attractive, they could already be in a relationship, or maybe they're simply not in the right mindset for dating. Either way, there are factors beyond your control. But when you create content and it falls flat, there's no denying that it's all on you.

Now imagine this happening after spending ten hours writing a post. Ten hours of your time and no one cares. Imagine this happening after you decided to leave a five-year relationship because your partner didn't support your work. Maybe she was right that your blog wasn't that good to begin with. Imagine this rejection piling up week . . . after week . . . after week and hearing mostly silence. So I became a rejection connoisseur, a master of silence. Mentally, this was the hardest period of my life.

However, by late 2017, things began to change. I met with some established financial writers at an investing conference, and they gave me the confidence to push onward. A few months later, I pitched myself to a few of them who had founded a wealth management firm in New York City. I wanted to align my day job with my interests. Thankfully, my pitch worked.

In early 2018, I left my first job and entered the world of financial services as a data scientist. I had been working full time for six years and was now firmly in Level 3 of the Wealth Ladder. The best part was that I was in an industry I was passionate about and was actively encouraged to keep writing. It was a win-win.

However, the move to New York City took a slight toll on my finances. Though my blog audience was still growing, my wealth had stagnated. The much higher cost of living in NYC made it hard for me to save money. But in 2020, everything changed.

COVID-19 hit and the stock market started to plummet. People were trapped inside and there wasn't much else to do besides go on the internet. As a result, the page views on my blog went through the roof. As the saying goes, "The higher the VIX, the higher the clicks." The VIX is a popular index of market volatility that reached a high of 85 in March 2020. And as predicted, the clicks came rolling in. Within a month my page views had tripled.

A few months prior to that, I had decided to start running web ads on my blog to make some extra income. By that point I had spent over 1,500 hours writing and had published 156 blog posts. Every Sunday for three years I wrote an article, and every Tuesday I gave it away for free. After amassing 1.6 million page views in those three years, I thought it was about time I started earning something from my work. However, I didn't want to have paid subscribers and lock up my content behind a paywall. Limiting access to something that I genuinely believed could help people with their finances didn't seem like the right move. I wanted everyone to be able to read and learn from my work. As a result, web ads seemed like the best solution. Before I knew it, I was making real money off something that I had previously given away. I had a legitimate online business now.

This was the beginning of my gradual ascent toward Level 4. Over the next few years, my audience grew, I took on new ad partnerships, and I wrote my first book, which became a bestseller. All the while I was taking the profits from my business and reinvesting them into income-producing assets. Thankfully, the markets obliged. In 2021 I made more from my investments than what I saved in my first three years of working.

It was mind-boggling to see how quickly my wealth could grow once I had a sizable amount invested. Of course, watching my wealth decline by roughly the same amount in 2022 wasn't easy, but thankfully, markets eventually recovered.

As I expanded my business on the weekends, during the week I was still working my full-time job. And while my job or my business *by themselves* wouldn't have allowed me to build wealth quickly, having them both at the same time was a game changer. I was following a Level 4 strategy before I had defined what a Level 4 strategy was. In particular, I was using leverage in the form of content to separate my time from my income. I would publish a blog post in the morning that would earn me money throughout the day and when I slept at night. I didn't have to put in more effort to earn more money. The leverage did it for me. I followed this playbook for half a decade.

And it worked. After twelve years of full-time employment and a side business for four of those years, I reached Level 4 at age thirty-four. No big inheritance. No IPOs. No 10x investments. Just a little over a decade of hard work, a high income, and some favorable stock market returns.

Looking back now, my journey up the Wealth Ladder can be defined by a few inflection points. A handful of moments that eventually got me to the next wealth level. The first was when I went into résumé-building mode in my sophomore year of college. That ensured I got a good job after graduation to get me into Level 2. The next was pushing myself in my early twenties to build my data/programming skills and raise my income. That's how I managed to get into Level 3. Lastly was realizing that my first job in litigation consulting was a dead end, so I started blogging. This transformed my career and gave me a side hustle that propelled me into Level 4 more quickly than I otherwise would have.

When I think about these inflection points as I climbed the Wealth Ladder, they didn't seem like inflection points at the time. As Steve Jobs said in his 2005 commencement address at Stanford University, "You can't connect the dots looking forward; you can only connect them looking backward. So you have to trust that the dots will somehow connect in your future."[2] I got lucky that my dots connected. Unfortunately, I didn't have a framework like the Wealth Ladder to guide my decision making along the way. I didn't know that I should change up my strategy as I gained wealth. I just happened to make the right choices around the right times.

I could easily imagine a world where my friend Michael never asks me about my sophomore internship and I never get the experience to put together a quality résumé. Then I never get that first internship, which never gets me my first job, and so forth. Long story short, change a few small things and you aren't reading this book right now. I know this is true because all this almost didn't happen.

A year after Michael taught me about the internship game, I was struggling to find an internship for the summer before my senior year of college. I applied to a handful of places, but once again, never made it past the résumé stage. Though I had worked as a research assistant during the previous summer, it wasn't enough to get an interview. The competition was too tough. No company would talk to me.

Unrelatedly, I went to see Dr. Jay Bhattacharya, my health economics professor, to discuss a paper I was writing for his class. We were scheduled to meet at 2:00 p.m., but when I arrived at his office, he wasn't there. I watched the minutes tick by as I sat there alone and 2:05 came and went. At 2:10 he was still nowhere to be found. I was about to get up and leave but decided that I should give him a few more minutes. Thankfully, he showed up at 2:13.

We discussed my paper, and near the end of our conversation he asked me, "What are you doing this summer?" I told him I planned to go work at a warehouse moving boxes where my aunt worked since I hadn't found an internship. He immediately replied, "No, you aren't doing that. Send me your résumé." Professor Bhattacharya then proceeded to tell me about a health-care consulting firm that was run by another Stanford professor. He said the internship would help me build my technical skills. So I went home and sent him my résumé, which he forwarded to the company. That company called me in for an interview, and I got the internship. That internship led me to my first job, which led me here.

All of this happened partially by chance. If I didn't wait those extra three minutes to see my professor, I have no clue where I would be today. Of course, luck will influence many parts of your life, but what you do with that luck matters more. Yes, I got rejected by a lot of places in college, but I also tried to capitalize on every opportunity I was given. As someone who came from a working-class background (i.e., Level 2), I never imagined I'd be where I am today. But getting to where I am isn't out of reach for the typical person. While you may not get there in your mid-thirties, it's still attainable for many. It reminds me of what Stephen A. Smith, a prominent sports television personality, said on ESPN's *First Take* in May 2014:

Everybody can't be Jay-Z. That's one in a billion. Everybody can't be Shaq and Kobe. That's one in a billion. But you can be Stephen A. Smith.[3]

You can be Nick Maggiulli too. While your journey won't look exactly like mine, there is a path out there for you that echoes mine. It might start in your late thirties instead of your early twenties. It might involve a full-time business instead of a side hustle. It might require a more demanding career or a different mix of investments. Either way, it's out there. You just have to find it.

Getting to Level 5 or Level 6 isn't easy. Many who make it there are incredibly skilled, come from exceptional backgrounds, and have their fair share of good luck. Mark Zuckerberg and Jeff Bezos are two such individuals who come to mind. But getting to Level 3 or Level 4 isn't out of the question. Many can make it there through hard work, career planning, and some good investments. I did it and I know you can too.

And it doesn't matter what you did previously. You can spend years feeling like you wasted your life, but if you can suddenly turn things around, you can completely rewrite your story and change your perspective. You can see yourself in a whole new light. After all, your past is ultimately defined by your present. It's not a fixed, immutable thing. It's just a memory inside your head. So if you can change your present, then you will change the interpretation of your past.

When I was getting rejected from every internship in college, I could've accepted that I didn't have the right connections, the right experience, or that I wasn't as smart as my peers. But I didn't. I kept applying and trying to improve myself. And even though all those beliefs about my shortcomings may have been true *at the time*, they aren't true now. None of those prior failures matter anymore, because I was able to find my own version of success. You can do the same. You can start following the strategies that will get you to Level 3 or Level 4.

And if you didn't grow up in Level 3 or Level 4, getting there can fundamentally change your life. My view of money has changed drastically as I've climbed the Wealth Ladder. I still remember sneaking miniature liquor bottles into a music festival in 2012 because I didn't want to pay nine dollars for a beer. Today, if my sister's car breaks down and she doesn't have money for the repair, I can send her whatever she needs.

My relationship with money has gone through a huge transformation over the past decade. I used to view money as a scarce resource that needed to be preserved. Now I see it as a tool to live a better life for myself and those around me. I am thankful every day that I can help my family when they're in need. It's truly a privilege. This is something I wouldn't have been able to do as easily when I was in Level 2.

At the same time, building wealth has given me a better understanding of why money is such a relative concept. It's the hidden lesson of the Wealth Ladder. I say "hidden" because, until you've experienced it for yourself, it can be difficult to comprehend.

For example, when I was a kid, I used to watch reality shows where people would do ridiculous things for what seemed like a lot of money. At the time, the risk of public embarrassment for the chance to win $25,000 made sense. But as I've gained wealth, I've started to view this behavior as increasingly absurd. Why would you expose your personal life to millions of people for the equivalent of a few fancy vacations after taxes? It doesn't add up. Similarly, I never understood why wealthy people would expend so much effort trying to pay less in taxes. But as my tax rate went up, I started to get it. It's not you until it's you.

This is why money is a relative concept. Because how you feel about it will change as you get more of it. I know how incredibly out of touch this sounds, but once you've experienced it for yourself, it's hard to see things any other way.

Lastly, the most important lesson I've gleaned from the Wealth Ladder is how little your life is impacted by money once you have enough of it. Money matters a lot until it doesn't. The writer Lawrence Yeo has a related article titled "The Nothingness of Money." In it he argues that when faced with our own mortality, we quickly realize how little money actually matters. As Yeo wrote, "Money is a required pursuit for life, but a pointless pursuit upon death."[4]

While Yeo was talking about money in a broader context, the same thing applies as you move up the Wealth Ladder. As I've noted previously, as you gain wealth, the nonfinancial aspects of your life become amplified. This is true because money can't buy everything. Unfortunately, we only tend to realize this *after* we've gotten the money, not before. The great irony of getting wealthy is realizing that many of life's greatest pleasures are free. Hanging out with friends. Spending time with family. Having excellent health. Feeling good about yourself. None of these things explicitly require money. Nick Cammarata, a writer and AI researcher, came to a similar conclusion when discussing the experience of his friends who became wealthy. As he noted, his friends originally wanted money because they focused mostly on the things they couldn't afford. But after they became wealthy, they thought more about what they wanted and realized that their true desires were relatively inexpensive. So they ended up doing those inexpensive things and not needing the money they yearned for in the first place.[5]

It's a cruel irony that many don't learn this lesson until *after* they've spent so much time chasing wealth. Then again, it's hard to come to this realization at the beginning of your journey. Only after experiencing it for yourself can you see otherwise. It reminds me of what Daniel Levinson wrote in *The Seasons of a Man's Life*:

> One of the great paradoxes of human development is that we are required to make crucial choices before we have the knowledge, judgment, and self-understanding to choose wisely. Yet if we put off these choices until we truly feel ready, the delay may produce other, greater costs.[6]

I know what this feels like. I've made the mistake of chasing money without knowing any better. And I know why others make this mistake as well. Because money is easy to measure. Understanding what you want out of life isn't. You can't check the status of your relationships or your health like you can check your bank balance. As a result, we get deceived into maximizing the thing we can most easily quantify—our wealth. Ironically, by focusing so much on building wealth early in my career, I've come to realize the importance of all the nonfinancial aspects of life.

Anytime my friends visit New York City, I try to make time

to see them. I plan a trip with my mother and sister every Mother's Day. If my wife asks me to watch a movie after dinner, I don't tell her I can't because I need to work. I try to exercise every day no matter what I have going on. I've shifted my priorities to focus on all the things that money *can't* buy. Those are the things that will ultimately matter in the long run. You don't have to believe me though. Climb the Wealth Ladder and see for yourself.

Finding Simplicity
in Complexity

I have a question for you. Do you know how to find the area of a circle? If you're like me, your gut instinct is to remember the formula that you learned in geometry class years ago. And if you don't remember the formula, you'd probably just search for it online. Well, that formula is:

$$\text{Area of a circle} = \pi * \text{radius}^2$$

This is the easy way to find the area of a circle. It's easy because the ancient Greeks discovered π (3.14 . . .) and figured out the formula. But what if you didn't have π? What if you didn't have the formula? How would you do it then?

Well, the ancient Greeks also had a clever way to solve this problem, before π or the formula. They did it through approximation.

First, they would take a circle and fit a noncurved shape, like a square or a hexagon, inside it. In geometry this is known as "inscribing." For example, they might *inscribe* a square inside a circle like so:

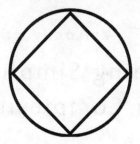

They would then find the area of this inner square (i.e., multiply the length by itself).

After that, they would take another square and fit it on the outside of the circle. This is known as "circumscribing" and would look something like this:

Once they had this, they would then find the area of this outer square.

Once they had the area of both the inner square and outer square, they could approximate the area of the circle. How so? Well, after finding the area of the two squares, they knew that the area of the circle had to be *between* these two values. After all, the circle is bigger than the inner square but smaller than the outer square. Therefore, its area must be bigger than the area of the inner square, but smaller than the area of the outer square.

You can see this more easily when we put the inner square, circle, and outer square all in the same image:

This is how the Greeks approximated the area of a circle before they had π or the formula.

But could they do better than a square? Yes. What if they inscribed a hexagon on the inside of the circle and circumscribed a hexagon on the outside of the circle? This is what that would look like:

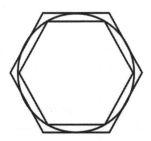

Now, the inner hexagon covers more area inside the circle than the inner square did. Additionally, the outer hexagon covers less area outside the circle than the other square did. In other words, the area of the inner hexagon is now closer to the area of the circle than the inner square was. And the area of the outer hexagon is closer to the area of the circle than the outer square was. As we went from a four-sided shape to a six-sided shape, our approximation got slightly better.

Now imagine repeating this process by adding more sides to the inner and outer noncurved shapes. After finding the area of the inner and outer hexagons, we can do the same thing with octagons. And after octagons, we can do decagons. And so forth. As we do this, the area of the inner shape and the area of the outer shape will approach the area of the circle. And, if we could draw an inner and outer shape with an infinite number of sides, then their areas would be virtually identical to the area of the circle. This method is known as exhaustion, and it demonstrates how the ancient Greeks solved a complex problem using a much simpler method.

Since the days of the ancient Greeks, the world has gotten far more complex. With the advent of the internet, information is spreading more rapidly now than during any other time in human history. On a daily basis Instagram gets 67 million new posts, Twitter/X produces about 500 million tweets, and Google gets 3.5 billion searches. Users add 720,000 hours of new video to YouTube each day.[1] That's equivalent to a full human lifetime (eighty-two years) uploaded to the platform on a daily basis.

But with this information abundance, a new problem has emerged. Whereas centuries ago we used to have trouble finding information, today the issue is filtering it. As the American historian Elizabeth Eisenstein once said, "There appears to be little reason to be concerned about 'the loss of mankind's memory.' There are good reasons for being concerned about the overloading of its circuits."[2] The challenge of the twenty-first century is not about getting information, but getting the right information. It's about finding the signal in the noise.

Thankfully, sometimes that signal is found in simpler ways than you might imagine. For example, despite having a reputation as one of the most technically talented hedge funds in history, Renaissance Technologies used many relatively simple methods to beat the market. Nick Patterson, PhD, a senior computational biologist, stated as much about his time working there:

> It's funny that I think the most important thing to do on data analysis is to do the simple things right. So, here's a kind of non-secret about what we did at Renaissance— in my opinion, our most important statistical tool was simple regression with one target and one independent variable. It's the simplest statistical model you can imagine. Any reasonably smart high school student could do it. Now we have some of the smartest people around working in our hedge fund. We have string theorists we recruited from Harvard and they're doing simple regression. Is this stupid and pointless? Should we be hiring stupider people and paying them less?
>
> And the answer is no. And the reason is nobody tells you what the variables you should be regressing [are]. What's the target? Should you do a nonlinear transform

before you regress? What's the source? Should you clean your data? Do you notice when your results are obviously rubbish? And so on. And the smarter you are the less likely you are to make a stupid mistake. And that's why I think you often need smart people who appear to be doing something technically very easy, but actually usually it's not so easy.[3]

Renaissance became one of the most profitable hedge funds in the world by finding simplicity in complexity. Unfortunately, most of the world isn't following Renaissance's model. Things are getting more complex, not less.

This book is an attempt at reversing this trend in our financial lives. The goal of the Wealth Ladder is to take the complicated world of wealth and provide a straightforward framework to view it through. It's meant to be a simple solution to one of the most complex problems in our lives—money.

This is why every wealth level has a singular thing for you to focus on if you want to keep climbing. In Level 1 it's safety. In Level 2 it's education. In Level 3 it's investing. In Level 4 it's starting a business. In Level 5 it's scaling a business. And in Level 6, it's protecting your wealth. But that's just the financial side of the Wealth Ladder. As I hope Part III has illustrated, wealth isn't about the money you've accumulated, but the life you've built with it.

So as we are bombarded with more information than we can ever hope to consume, how will we determine what's important and what isn't? I don't have all the answers. But when it comes to building wealth, I've tried doing my part.

Thank you for reading.

Acknowledgments

I would like to thank Carl Joseph-Black, Katie Gatti Tassin, Frazer Rice, and Nat Eliason for their feedback on earlier drafts of this book. Any brilliance found here is theirs. Any mistakes are my own. I'd like to thank my agent, David Fugate, for his patience and guidance from the earliest conception of the Wealth Ladder. He was essential to making this work possible.

I'd like to give a special shout-out to my fantastic editor, Noah Schwartzberg. Without him, this book would not exist. Noah, thank you for pushing me to write this for so many years, even when I felt like I wasn't ready. I'm glad I finally took you up on your offer.

I'd like to thank my beloved wife, Fjolla, for her unwavering support throughout the writing process. Thank you for giving me the time, space, and inspiration to follow my dreams. Life is so much better with you in it. I love you.

I'd like to thank my Nana and Papa, my mother, my father, and my sister for believing in me from the very beginning. You guys have always been in my corner, and I couldn't have asked for a better family to get me to where I am today.

Lastly, I'd like to thank all my readers for making this possible. I started writing in 2017 and didn't think anyone would ever care. But fortunately, some of you did. It's been a privilege and an honor. So once again, thank you.

NOTES

Introduction

1. Jeremy Goldman, "13 Insightful Quotes from Intel Visionary Andy Grove," *Inc.*, March 22, 2016, https://www.inc.com/jeremy -goldman/13-insightful-quotes-from-intel-visionary-andy-grove .html.

2. UBS, "Global Wealth Report 2024," UBS Global Wealth Management, July 2024, https://www.ubs.com/us/en/wealth -management/insights/global-wealth-report.html; Henley & Partners, Centi-Millionaire Report 2024, June 2024, https://www .henleyglobal.com/publications/centi-millionaire-report-2024.

3. Board of Governors of the Federal Reserve System, "Survey of Consumer Finances," last modified 2023, https://www .federalreserve.gov/econres/scfindex.htm; Henley & Partners, Centi-Millionaire Report 2024, June 2024, https://www .henleyglobal.com/publications/centi-millionaire-report-2024. Twenty-five percent of all interviews in the 2022 Survey of Consumer Finances were conducted between January and April 2023 (See: https://www.federalreserve.gov/publications/files/scf23 .pdf). Therefore, I referenced 2023 in the text for simplicity and consistency with the 2023 world data from the 2024 UBS Global Wealth Report.

Chapter 1: Spending up the Wealth Ladder

1. Pliny the Elder, *The Natural History*, Book IX, *The Natural History of Fishes*, Chapter 58, "Instances of the Use of Pearls," ed. John Bostock and H. T. Riley, http://data.perseus.org/citations /urn:cts:latinLit:phi0978.phi001.perseus-eng1:9.58

2. Fatih Guvenen, Fatih Karahan, Serdar Ozkan, and Jae Song, "What Do Data on Millions of U.S. Workers Reveal About Life-Cycle Earnings Risk?," Working Paper 20913, National Bureau of Economic Research, January 2015, http://www.nber.org/papers /w20913.

3. Karen Dynan, Douglas Elmendorf, and Daniel Sichel, "The Evolution of Household Income Volatility," *B.E. Journal of Economic Analysis & Policy* 12, no. 2 (2012), https://doi.org /10.1515/1935-1682.3347.

4. Christina Gough, "Average Sports Salaries by League," Statista, June 1, 2023, https://www.statista.com/statistics/675120/average -sports-salaries-by-league/.

Chapter 2: Earning up the Wealth Ladder

1. Panasonic Group, "Corporate History," https://holdings .panasonic/global/corporate/about/history/chronicle.html; "From Birth to the Founding of the Company," https://holdings .panasonic/global/corporate/about/history/chronicle/1894.html; "Panasonic Launched," https://holdings.panasonic/global /corporate/about/history/chronicle/1918.html.

2. "The 'God of Management' Explained How to Practice the Spirit of Capitalism," The Liberty Web, February 3, 2015, https://eng .the-liberty.com/2015/5649/; Karl Schoenberger, "Konosuke Matsushita; Japan Industrialist, Billionaire," *Los Angeles Times*, April 28, 1989, https://www.latimes.com/archives/la-xpm-1989 -04-28-mn-1905-story.html.

3. Eric Jorgenson, "How to Manage Opportunity Cost: Attention Thresholds in Personal Wealth Building," December 23, 2021, https://www.ejorgenson.com/blog/opportunity-cost-attention -thresholds.

4. Eric Jorgenson, "How to Manage Opportunity Cost,"

5. Board of Governors of the Federal Reserve System, "Survey of Consumer Finances," last modified 2023, https://www .federalreserve.gov/econres/scfindex.htm.

6. Bureau of Labor Statistics, "Table 7. Survival of Private Sector Establishments by Opening Year," last modified April 2024, https://www.bls.gov/bdm/us_age_naics_00_table7.txt.

7. Naval Ravikant, "Product and Media Are New Leverage," YouTube video, 5:18, April 17, 2019, https://youtube.com/watch ?v=GtyWqj2ESiQ&list=UUh_dVD10YuSghle8g6yjePg.

8. Fred Schwed Jr., *Where Are the Customers' Yachts?: Or a Good Hard Look at Wall Street* (Hoboken, NJ: Wiley, 2006).

9. Jack Butcher, X (formerly Twitter) post, February 4, 2021, 8:40 p.m., https://x.com/jackbutcher/status/1357549632361017346?s=20.

Chapter 3: Investing up the Wealth Ladder

1. Board of Governors of the Federal Reserve System, "Survey of Consumer Finances," last modified 2023, https://www .federalreserve.gov/econres/scfindex.htm.

2. Nick Maggiulli, *Just Keep Buying: Proven Ways to Save Money and Build Your Wealth* (Petersfield, NH: Harriman House, 2022).

Chapter 4: Level 1 (<$10k)

1. Mike Black, *Million Dollar Comeback*, YouTube video series, 2020–2021, https://www.youtube.com/playlist?list=PLsHj7wHXk _30MNctxxcB7oO68PCcw2WGQ.

2. William T. Vollmann, *Poor People* (New York: Ecco Press, 2008).

3. Kartik Athreya, José Mustre-del-Río, and Juan M. Sánchez, "The Persistence of Financial Distress," *Review of Financial Studies* 32, no. 10 (2019): 3851–83, https://doi.org/10.1093/rfs/hhz009.

4. David U. Himmelstein et al., "Medical Bankruptcy: Still Common Despite the Affordable Care Act," *American Journal of Public Health* 109, no. 3 (March 2019): 431–33, https://doi.org/10.2105/AJPH.2018.304901.

5. Warren Buffett, "Warren Buffett, Lecture, Nebraska Educational Forum, 1999," YouTube video, 59:39, Investor Archive, October 11, 1999, https://www.youtube.com/watch?v=HM9h9t1vpIE.

6. Board of Governors of the Federal Reserve System, "Survey of Consumer Finances," last modified 2023, https://www.federalreserve.gov/econres/scfindex.htm.

7. U.S. Bureau of Labor Statistics, "Consumer Expenditure Survey, 2022," U.S. Department of Labor, 2023, https://download.bls.gov/pub/time.series/cx/.

8. Jackson Gruver, "Biggest College Regrets," PayScale, June 25, 2019, https://www.payscale.com/research-and-insights/biggest-college-regrets/.

9. Ruby K. Payne, *A Framework for Understanding Poverty* (Highlands, TX: aha! Process, Inc., 2018), 49.

10. Daryl Collins et al., *Portfolios of the Poor: How the World's Poor Live on $2 a Day* (Princeton, NJ: Princeton University Press, 2010).

11. Chris Arnade, *Dignity: Seeking Respect in Back Row America* (New York: Sentinel, 2019).

Chapter 5: Level 2 ($10k–$100k)

1. "Trained to Be a Genius, Girl, 16, Wallops Chess Champ Spassky for $110,000," *Chicago Tribune*, February 18, 1993, https://www

.chicagotribune.com/1993/02/18/trained-to-be-a-genius-girl
-16-wallops-chess-champ-spassky-for-110000/.

2. "Best Paying Jobs," *U.S. News & World Report*, https://money
.usnews.com/careers/best-jobs/rankings/best-paying-jobs.

3. Board of Governors of the Federal Reserve System, "Survey
of Consumer Finances," last modified 2023, https://www
.federalreserve.gov/econres/scfindex.htm.

4. Adam Looney and Constantine Yannelis, "A Crisis in Student
Loans?: How Changes in the Characteristics of Borrowers and in
the Institutions They Attended Contributed to Rising Loan
Defaults," *Brookings Papers on Economic Activity* 2015, no. 2
(2015): 1–89.

5. Food and Agriculture Organization of the United Nations (FAO),
World Food and Agriculture—Statistical Yearbook 2023 (Rome:
FAO, 2023), https://doi.org/10.4060/cc8166en.

6. Paul Graham, "How to Do Great Work," *Paul Graham* (blog),
July 2023, https://paulgraham.com/greatwork.html.

7. James Donaldson, interviewed by Joe Rogan, "Mr.Beast," *The Joe
Rogan Experience* (podcast), March 7, 2022, https://open.spotify
.com/episode/5lokpznqvSrJO3gButgQvs.

8. Nicolas Vega, "MrBeast Brings in $700 Million a Year but Says
He's Not Rich: 'I've Reinvested Everything to the Point of
Stupidity,'" CNBC, February 15, 2024, https://www.cnbc.com
/2024/02/15/mrbeast-brings-in-700-million-a-yearheres-why
-he-says-hes-not-rich.html.

9. Scott Galloway, *The Algebra of Wealth* (New York: Portfolio
/Penguin, 2024), 60.

10. Board of Governors of the Federal Reserve System, "Survey
of Consumer Finances," last modified 2023, https://www
.federalreserve.gov/econres/scfindex.htm.

11. "Sam Altman: How to Build the Future," *Y Combinator* (podcast), YouTube video, September 27, 2016, https://www.youtube.com/watch?v=sYMqVwsewSg.

Chapter 6: Level ($100k–$1M)

1. Gary Flandro, "Fast Reconnaissance Missions to the Outer Solar System Utilizing Energy Derived from the Gravitational Field of Jupiter" (PDF), *Astronautica Acta*, 12, no. 4 (1966): 329–37, http://www.gravityassist.com/IAF3-2/Ref.%203-143.pdf.

2. Nick Maggiulli, "Go Big, Then Stop," *Of Dollars And Data* (blog), July 27, 2021, https://ofdollarsanddata.com/go-big-then-stop/.

3. "William Preston Lane Jr. Memorial (Bay) Bridge (US 50/301)," Maryland Transportation Authority, https://mdta.maryland.gov/Toll_Facilities/WPL.html.

4. Trip Gabriel, "Quelling Anxiety Across the Chesapeake," *New York Times*, May 26, 2013, https://www.nytimes.com/2013/05/27/us/service-aids-fearful-drivers-across-the-chesapeake.html.

5. "Meet Twiggy, the Globe-Trotting Squirrel," Twiggy's Inc., https://twiggysinc.com/#about/.

6. Panel Study of Income Dynamics, public use dataset, produced and distributed by the Survey Research Center, Institute for Social Research, University of Michigan, Ann Arbor, MI, 2024.

7. Panel Study of Income Dynamics, public use dataset.

8. Panel Study of Income Dynamics, public use dataset.

Chapter 7: Level 4 ($1M–$10M)

1. Robert Trumbull, "World's Richest Little Isle," *New York Times*, March 7, 1982, https://www.nytimes.com/1982/03/07/magazine/world-s-richest-little-isle.html.

2. *Asian Development Outlook 2005* (Hong Kong: Asian Development Bank, 2005), 204–6, available at https://www.adb.org/sites/default /files/publication/27713/ado2005.pdf.

3. Peter Dauvergne, "A Dark History of the World's Smallest Island Nation," *MIT Press Reader*, July 22, 2019, https://thereader .mitpress.mit.edu/dark-history-nauru/.

4. Noah Kagan, X (formerly Twitter) post, December 18, 2023, 4:19 p.m., https://x.com/noahkagan/status/1736858651351032311 ?s=20.

5. Amy C. Arnott, "15 Funds That Have Destroyed the Most Wealth over the Past Decade," Morningstar, February 2, 2024, https:// www.morningstar.com/funds/15-funds-that-have-destroyed-most -wealth-over-past-decade.

6. *Succession*, season 2, episode 9, "DC," October 6, 2019, HBO.

7. Marshall Goldsmith, *What Got You Here Won't Get You There: How Successful People Become Even More Successful* (New York: Hyperion, 2007).

8. Felix Dennis, *How to Get Rich* (New York: Portfolio/Penguin, 2008), 170.

9. Board of Governors of the Federal Reserve System, "Survey of Consumer Finances," last modified 2023, https://www .federalreserve.gov/econres/scfindex.htm.

10. Jim Taylor, Doug Harrison, and Stephen Kraus, *The New Elite: Inside the Minds of the Truly Wealthy* (New York: AMACOM, 2009), 42.

11. Alfred North Whitehead, *An Introduction to Mathematics* (1911; Project Gutenberg, 2012), 46, https://www.gutenberg.org /files/41568/41568-pdf.pdf.

12. "Elon Musk, 'Starting a Company Is Like EATING GLASS . . . ,'" YouTube video, July 31, 2023, https://www.youtube.com/watch ?v=5r4JXqovL54.

13. "NVIDIA CEO Jensen Huang," *Acquired* (podcast), YouTube video, October 15, 2023, https://www.youtube.com/watch?v =y6NfxiemvHg.

14. Benjamin F. Jones and Daniel Kim, "Most Successful Entrepreneurs Are Older Than You Think," Clifford-Lewis Private Wealth, February 11, 2023, https://www.clifford-lewis.com /blog/most-successful-entrepreneurs-are-older-than-you-think.

15. Jones and Kim, "Most Successful Entrepreneurs Are Older Than You Think."

16. Comment on "Entrepreneurs Aren't a Special Breed—They're Mostly Rich Kids," Hacker News, November 9, 2017, https://news .ycombinator.com/item?id=15659076.

17. Zev Stub, "Parents' Income, Not Smarts, Key to Entrepreneurship—Study," *Jerusalem Post*, January 28, 2021, https://www.jpost.com/israel-news/parents-income-not-smarts -key-to-entrepreneurship-study-657058.

18. Gene Marks, "Entrepreneurs Are Great, but It's Mom and Dad Who Gave Them Their Start," *The Guardian*, January 31, 2021, https://www.theguardian.com/business/2021/jan/31/small -business-entrepreneurs-success-parents.

19. Michael E. Gerber, *The E-Myth Revisited: Why Most Small Businesses Don't Work and What to Do About It* (New York: HarperCollins, 1995), chapter 3.

Chapter 8: Level 5 ($10M–$100M)

1. Jordan O'Connor, X (formerly Twitter) post, December 13, 2023, 8:53 a.m., https://x.com/jdnoc/status/1734934564928196841.

2. Jon Swartz, "Losing's Not an Option for Cuban," *USA Today*, April 25, 2004, https://usatoday30.usatoday.com/money /2004-04-25-cuban_x.htm; Jeremy Salvucci, "Mark Cuban's Net Worth: 'Shark Tank' Departure," TheStreet, January 23, 2024, https://www.thestreet.com/investing/mark-cuban-net-worth -career-investments.

3. Daniel Rugunya, "Zip2—Elon Musk's First Successful Startup," TechieGamers, January 12, 2024, https://techiegamers.com/zip2 -elon-musk/.

4. Michelle Conlin, "Netflix: Flex to the Max," *BusinessWeek*, September 23, 2007, https://web.archive.org/web/20120809073023 /http://www.businessweek.com/stories/2007-09-23/netflix-flex -to-the-max.

5. Charles E. Eesley and Edward B. Roberts, "Cutting Your Teeth: The Beginning of the Learning Curve," paper presented at the 2009 Portland International Conference on Management of Engineering & Technology, Portland, Oregon, August 2–6, 2009.

6. Aileen Lee, "Welcome to the Unicorn Club: Learning from Billion-Dollar Startups," TechCrunch, November 2, 2013, https:// techcrunch.com/2013/11/02/welcome-to-the-unicorn-club/.

7. Shannon P. Pratt, *The Market Approach to Valuing Businesses* (New York: Wiley, 2000), 252.

8. Lee, "Welcome To The Unicorn Club: Learning From Billion- Dollar Startups."

9. Erin McDowell, "These 10 Billionaires Have All Gone Broke or Declared Bankruptcy—Read the Wild Stories of How They Lost Their Fortunes," *Business Insider*, March 26, 2020, https://www .businessinsider.com/rich-billionaires-who-declared-bankruptcy -2019-7.

10. Frazer Rice, *Wealth, Actually: Intelligent Decision-Making for the 1%* (Austin, TX: Lioncrest Publishing, 2018), 243.

11. Andrew S. Grove, *Only the Paranoid Survive: How to Exploit the Crisis Points That Challenge Every Company* (New York: Crown Business, 1999).

12. Bill Dedman, "At 104, the Mysterious Heiress Huguette Clark Is Alone Now," NBC News, August 19, 2010, https://via.hypothes .is/https://www.nbcnews.com/id/wbna38719231; Adam Martin, "Inside Huguette Clark's Massive Homes," *The Atlantic*, June 1, 2011, https://www.theatlantic.com/national/archive/2011/06 /inside-houses-huguette-clark/351324/; Bill Dedman, "Huguette Clark's $300 Million Copper Fortune Is Divided Up: Here's the Deal," NBC News, September 24, 2013, https://www.nbcnews .com/news/world/huguette-clarks-300-million-copper-fortune -divided-heres-deal-flna4b11244681; Bill Dedman, "Family Excluded from Huguette Clark Burial," NBC News, May 26, 2011, https://www.nbcnews.com/id/wbna43166747.

13. Clay Cockrell, "I'm a Therapist to the Super-Rich: They Are as Miserable as Succession Makes Out," *The Guardian*, November 22, 2021, https://www.theguardian.com/commentisfree/2021 /nov/22/therapist-super-rich-succession-billionaires.

14. Lee Ying Shan, "'Wealth Can Be Pretty Isolating': Problems That Rich People Face, According to Therapists," CNBC, May 13, 2024, https://www.cnbc.com/2024/05/14/problems-that-rich -people-face-according-to-therapists-.html.

15. Thomas C. Corley, "I Studied 177 Self-Made Millionaires for 5 Years, and Learned That Rich People Deliberately Surround Themselves with Rich Friends. Here Are the Traits to Look For to Do the Same," *Business Insider*, February 21, 2020, https:// www.businessinsider.com/rich-people-choose-friends-differently -2018-1.

16. Rui Zhang et al., "Household Wealth and Individuals' Mental Health: Evidence from the 2012–2018 China Family Panel Survey," *International Journal of Environmental Research and Public Health* 19, no. 18 (September 14, 2022): 11569, https://doi.org/10.3390/ijerph191811569.

17. Arthur T. Vanderbilt II, *Fortune's Children: The Fall of the House of Vanderbilt* (New York: William Morrow, 2013), 111–12.

18. Suniya S. Luthar and Karen D'Avanzo, "Contextual Factors in Substance Use: A Study of Suburban and Inner-City Adolescents," *Development and Psychopathology* 11, no. 4 (Fall 1999): 845–67, https://doi.org/10.1017/s0954579499002357; Suniya S. Luthar, "The Culture of Affluence: Psychological Costs of Material Wealth," *Child Development* 74, no. 6 (November 2003): 1581–93, https://doi.org/10.1046/j.1467-8624.2003.00625.x.

19. Suniya S. Luthar and Bronwyn E. Becker, "Privileged but Pressured? A Study of Affluent Youth," *Child Development* 73, no. 5 (September–October 2002): 1593–1610, https://doi.org/10.1111/1467-8624.00492.

20. Christopher P. Salas-Wright et al., "Substance Use Disorders Among First- and Second-Generation Immigrant Adults in the United States: Evidence of an Immigrant Paradox?," *Journal of Studies on Alcohol and Drugs* 75, no. 6 (2014): 958–67, https://doi.org/10.15288/jsad.2014.75.958.

21. Business Wire, "Comments by Warren E. Buffett in Conjunction with His Annual Contribution of Berkshire Hathaway Shares to Five Foundations," June 23, 2021, https://www.businesswire.com/news/home/20210623005262/en/.

22. Alex Hormozi, LinkedIn post, https://www.linkedin.com/posts/alexhormozi_the-life-you-want-is-on-the-other-side-of-activity-7105928499927891968-Pyry/.

Chapter 9: Level 6 ($100M+)

1. Hourly History, *Alfred Nobel: A Life from Beginning to End*, independently published, 2020, ebook.

2. "Alfred Nobel's Will," NobelPrize.org, Nobel Prize Outreach AB, https://www.nobelprize.org/alfred-nobel/alfred-nobels-will/; "Alfred Nobel's Fortune," Norwegian Nobel Institute, https://www.nobelpeaceprize.org/nobel-peace-prize/history/alfred-nobel-s-fortune; Nathan Reiff, "Where Does the Nobel Prize Money Come From?," Investopedia, April 19, 2024, https://www.investopedia.com/news/where-does-nobel-prize-money-come/.

3. Morgan Housel, "A Few Laws of Getting Rich," *Collaborative Fund* (blog), October 15, 2023, https://collabfund.com/blog/a-few-laws-of-getting-rich/.

4. James J. Sexton, *How to Stay in Love: Practical Wisdom from an Unexpected Source* (New York: Henry Holt and Co., 2018), 21.

5. Michelle Quinn, "Success, Bankruptcy . . . Suicide," *New York Times*, September 26, 1993, https://www.nytimes.com/1993/09/26/business/success-bankruptcy-suicide.html; Associated Press, "Roy Raymond, 47; Began Victoria's Secret," *New York Times*, September 2, 1993, https://www.nytimes.com/1993/09/02/obituaries/roy-raymond-47-began-victoria-s-secret.html.

6. Marvin Schwartz, "Estimates of Personal Wealth, 1982: A Second Look," Internal Revenue Service, ttps://www.irs.gov/pub/irs-soi/82pwesl.pdf.

7. Misha Saul, "We Are Made to Live Like Firemen," Kvetch, November 13, 2022, https://www.kvetch.au/p/we-are-made-to-live-like-firemen.

8. "Full Transcript from CNBC's 'Charlie Munger: A Life of Wit and Wisdom,'" CNBC, November 30, 2023, https://www.cnbc.com/amp/2023/11/30/full-transcript-from-cnbcs-charlie-munger-a-life-of-wit-and-wisdom-.html.

9. "30-Year Journey from Tribal Boy to Forest Man," *Times of India*, August 3, 2014, https://timesofindia.indiatimes.com/home /environment/developmental-issues/30-year-journey-from-tribal -boy-to-Forest-Man/articleshow/39510215.cms.

Chapter 10: How Long Does It Take to Climb the Wealth Ladder?

1. Casey Wolfington, "Wolfington: The Power of Hope," Vail Health Behavioral Health, March 20, 2020, https://www .vailhealthbh.org/about/news/wolfington-the-power-of-hope.

2. Board of Governors of the Federal Reserve System, "Survey of Consumer Finances," last modified 2023, https://www .federalreserve.gov/econres/scfindex.htm.

3. Panel Study of Income Dynamics, public use dataset, produced and distributed by the Survey Research Center, Institute for Social Research, University of Michigan, Ann Arbor, MI, 2024.

4. World Bank, "Ending Extreme Poverty: Progress, but Uneven and Slowing," in *Poverty and Shared Prosperity 2018: Piecing Together the Poverty Puzzle* (Washington, DC: World Bank, 2018), 19–46, https://openknowledge.worldbank.org/server/api /core/bitstreams/77abe096-59b7-5688-92cf-21584314b380 /content.

Chapter 11: Does Money Buy Happiness?

1. Daniel Kahneman and Angus Deaton, "High Income Improves Evaluation of Life but Not Emotional Well-Being," *Proceedings of the National Academy of Sciences* 107, no. 38 (September 7, 2010): 16489–93, https://doi.org/10.1073/pnas.1011492107.

2. Matthew A. Killingsworth, "Experienced Well-Being Rises with Income, Even Above $75,000 per Year," *Proceedings of the National Academy of Sciences* 118, no. 4 (January 18, 2021): e2016976118, https://doi.org/10.1073/pnas.2016976118.

3. Matthew A. Killingsworth, Daniel Kahneman, and Barbara Mellers, "Income and Emotional Well-Being: A Conflict Resolved," *Proceedings of the National Academy of Sciences* 120, no. 10 (March 7, 2023): e2208661120, https://doi.org/10.1073 /pnas.2208661120.

4. Killingsworth, Kahneman, and Mellers, "Income and Emotional Well-Being: A Conflict Resolved."

5. Matthew A. Killingsworth, "Money and Happiness: Extended Evidence Against Satiation," *Happiness Science*, July 17, 2024, https://happiness-science.org/money-happiness-satiation.

6. Elizabeth W. Dunn, Lara B. Aknin, and Michael I. Norton, "Spending Money on Others Promotes Happiness," *Science* 319, no. 5870 (March 21, 2008): 1687–88.

7. Emily Peck, "The Richer You Are, the More Money You Need to Be Happy," *Axios*, December 1, 2023, https://www.axios.com /2023/12/01/money-needed-to-be-happy-wealth.

8. Mihaly Csikszentmihalyi, "If We Are So Rich, Why Aren't We Happy?," *American Psychologist* 54, no. 10 (October 1999): 821–27.

9. Anne Lamott, "Let Us Commence," *Salon*, June 6, 2003, https:// www.salon.com/2003/06/06/commencement/.

10. Nick Maggiulli, "The Never-Ending Then," *Of Dollars And Data* (blog), September 12, 2023, https://ofdollarsanddata.com/the -never-ending-then/.

11. Lucía Macchia and Ashley V. Whillans, "Leisure Beliefs and the Subjective Well-Being of Nations," *Journal of Positive Psychology* 16, no. 2 (2021): 198–206.

12. Felix Dennis, *How to Get Rich* (New York: Portfolio/Penguin, 2008), 6.

13. Robert Frank, "How to be 'Comfortably Poor' on $3 Million," *Wall Street Journal*, March 17, 2010, https://www.wsj.com/articles /BL-WHB-2831.

14. Dennis, *How to Get Rich*, 23.

Chapter 12: The Great Enhancer

1. Samin Nosrat, *Salt, Fat, Acid, Heat: Mastering the Elements of Good Cooking* (New York: Simon and Schuster, 2017), 46.

2. Sahil Bloom, X (formerly Twitter) post, June 26, 2022, 9:48 a.m., https://x.com/SahilBloom/status/1541055681356234752.

3. Tracey Camilleri, Samantha Rockey, and Robin Dunbar, *The Social Brain: The Psychology of Successful Groups* (London: Penguin Books, 2023), 67.

4. Alexandra Thompson, Michael A. Smith, Andrew McNeill, and Thomas V. Pollet, "Friendships, Loneliness and Psychological Wellbeing in Older Adults: A Limit to the Benefit of the Number of Friends," *Ageing & Society* 44, no. 5 (2024): 1090–115, https://doi .org/10.1017/S0144686X22000666.

5. Matthew D. Lieberman, *Social: Why Our Brains Are Wired to Connect* (New York: Crown, 2013), 247.

6. Irwin Abrams, *The Nobel Peace Prize and the Laureates* (Nantucket Island, MA: Watson Publishing International, 2001).

7. Lara B. Aknin and Gillian M. Sandstrom, "People Are Surprisingly Hesitant to Reach Out to Old Friends," *Communications Psychology* 2, no. 1 (2024): 34, https://doi.org/10.1038/s44271 -024-00075-8.

8. John Waters, "John Waters Commencement Address—RISD 2015," Vimeo video, 12:20, May 30, 2015, https://vimeo.com /129312307.

9. Emily Batdorf, "Survey: What Role Does Money Play in Romantic Relationships?," Forbes Advisor, January 26, 2024, https://
    download.bls.gov/pub/time.series/cx/.

10. Alexandra Killewald, Angela Lee, and Paula England, "Wealth
    and Divorce," *Demography* 60, no. 1 (January 2023): 147–71,
    https://doi.org/10.1215/00703370-10413021.

11. "What Makes Life Meaningful? Views from 17 Advanced
    Economies," Pew Research Center, November 18, 2021, https://
    www.pewresearch.org/global/2021/11/18/finding-meaning
    -in-what-one-does/.

12. Dorothy Sayers, "Why Work?," in *Letters to a Diminished Church*
    (1942; Nashville, TN: Thomas Nelson, 2004), https://www1
    .villanova.edu/dam/villanova/mission/faith/Why%20Work
    %20by%20Dorothy%20Sayers.pdf.

13. Jørn Winther, *Frost/Nixon: The Complete Interviews* (Los
    Angeles: Syndicast Services, May 4–September 10, 1977),
    television broadcast.

14. Ernie J. Zelinski, *How to Retire Happy, Wild, and Free* (Edmonton,
    AB: Visions International Publishing, 2013), 24.

15. Robert M. Sapolsky, *Why Zebras Don't Get Ulcers* (New York:
    Holt Paperbacks, 2004), 5–6.

16. Mary Worthen and Elizabeth Cash, *Stress Management* (Treasure
    Island, FL: StatPearls Publishing, 2023), http://www.ncbi.nlm
    .nih.gov/books/NBK513300/.

17. Sapolsky, *Why Zebras Don't Get Ulcers*, 363.

18. Lieberman, *Social: Why Our Brains Are Wired to Connect*, 247.

19. Justin Yang et al., "Association Between Push-up Exercise
    Capacity and Future Cardiovascular Events Among Active Adult

Men," *JAMA Network Open* 2, no. 2 (2019): e188341, https://doi
.org/10.1001/jamanetworkopen.2018.8341.

20. Hongwei Ji et al., "Sex Differences in Association of Physical
    Activity with All-Cause and Cardiovascular Mortality," *Journal
    of the American College of Cardiology* 83, no. 8 (2024): 783–93,
    https://doi.org/10.1016/j.jacc.2023.12.019.

21. Andrew Huberman, "Dr. Peter Attia: Exercise, Nutrition,
    Hormones for Vitality & Longevity," *Huberman Lab* (podcast),
    YouTube video, 2:50:02, August 15, 2022, https://www.youtube
    .com/watch?v=DTCmprPCDqc.

22. Michael G. Marmot, Geoffrey Rose, Martin Shipley, and P. J. S.
    Hamilton, "Employment Grade and Coronary Heart Disease in
    British Civil Servants," *Journal of Epidemiology and Community
    Health* 32, no. 4 (1978): 244–49, https://doi.org/10.1136/jech.32.4.244.

23. Michael Daly, Christopher Boyce, and Alex Wood, "A Social
    Rank Explanation of How Money Influences Health," *Health
    Psychology* 34, no. 3 (2015): 222, https://doi.org/10.1037/hea0000098.

24. Alexandr Kopytov, Nikolai Roussanov, and Mathieu Taschereau-
    Dumouchel, "Cheap Thrills: The Price of Leisure and the Global
    Decline in Work Hours," *Journal of Political Economy Macroeco-
    nomics* 1, no. 1 (2023): 80–118, https://doi.org/10.1086/723717.

25. Zelinski, *How to Retire Happy, Wild, and Free*, 16.

26. Lucius Annaeus Seneca, "On the Shortness of Life," in *Dialogues
    and Letters*, trans. C. D. N. Costa (London: Penguin Books,
    2005), 1.

Chapter 13: My Journey up the Wealth Ladder

1. Chris Clark, "'You Gotta Do It': The Late Charlie Munger Once
   Said Your First $100K Is the Toughest to Earn," Yahoo Finance,

November 29, 2023, https://finance.yahoo.com/news/b-gotta
-charlie-munger-says-140000516.html.

2. Steve Jobs, "Steve Jobs' 2005 Stanford Commencement Address,"
   June 12, 2005, YouTube video, 15:04, March 7, 2008, https://www
   .youtube.com/watch?v=UF8uR6Z6KLc.

3. Stephen A. Smith, "Stephen A. Smith Going Off on ESPN About
   the American Dream," YouTube video, excerpt from *First Take*,
   ESPN, May 23, 2014, https://www.youtube.com/watch?v=n
   _mdB07gtfU.

4. Lawrence Yeo, "The Nothingness of Money," *More To That*
   (blog), 2021, https://moretothat.com/the-nothingness-of-money/.

5. Nick Cammarata, X (formerly Twitter) post, January 19, 2024,
   5:17 p.m., https://x.com/nickcammarata/status/17484697714637
   94976.

6. Daniel J. Levinson, *The Seasons of a Man's Life* (New York:
   Ballantine Books, 1986), 102.

Epilogue: Finding Simplicity in Complexity

1. "Breaking Down the Numbers: How Much Data Does the World
   Create Daily in 2024?," *Edge Delta* (blog), March 11, 2024, https://
   edgedelta.com/company/blog/how-much-data-is-created-per-day.

2. James Gleick, *The Information: A History, a Theory, a Flood*
   (New York: Pantheon, 2011), 401.

3. "AI Safety and the Legacy of Bletchley Park," Talking Machines,
   February 25, 2016, https://www.thetalkingmachines.com
   /episodes/ai-safety-and-legacy-bletchley-park.